D0870163

The

Lyric Theatre

presents

THREE SISTERS

by Lucy Caldwell

in a version of the play by
Anton Chekhov

Directed by Selina Cartmell

First performed at the Lyric Theatre, Belfast,
on Saturday 15 October 2016

*Generously supported by the Belfast International
Arts Festival*

Cast

in order of appearance

Siu Jing	**Shin-Fei Chen**
Erin	**Amy Blair**
Marianne	**Christine Clare**
Orla	**Julie Maxwell**
Beattie	**Niall Cusack**
Baron	**Lewis MacKinnon**
Simon	**Julian Moore-Cook**
Vershinin	**Tim Treloar**
Andy	**Aidan O'Neill**
DJ Cool	**Patrick McBrearty**
Rod	**Matthew Forsythe**
Teddy	**Gerard Jordan**

Creative Team

Writer	**Lucy Caldwell,** after **Anton Chekhov**
Director	**Selina Cartmell**
Set and Costume Designer	**Alex Lowde**
Lighting Designer	**Ciaran Bagnall**
Composer and Sound Designer	**Isobel Waller-Bridge**
Movement Director	**Dylan Quinn**
Vocal Coach	**Brendan Gunn**
Assistant Director	**Louisa Sanfey**
Literal Translator	**Helen Rappaport**

Production Team

Production Manager	**Alan McCracken**
Technical Manager	**Keith Ginty**
Technician	**Tighearnan O'Neill**
Set Builder	**Peter Lorimer**
Carpenter and Set Builder	**Noel Woods**
Casting	**Clare Gault**
Casting Adviser	**Annelie Powell**
Company Stage Manager	**Kate Miller**
Deputy Stage Manager	**Tracey Lindsay**
Assistant Stage Manager	**Louise Bryans**
Stage Management Interns	**Gina Donnelly** and **Stephanie Dale**
Wardrobe Supervisor	**Enda Kenny**
Wardrobe Assistant	**Erin Charteris**
Costume Assistants	**Niamh Kearney** and **Una Hickey**
Hair and Make-Up	**Orlaith Walsh**

Amy Blair | *Erin*

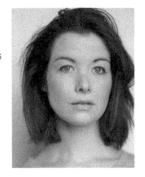

Amy trained at the Guildford School of Acting, graduating in 2014. Theatre credits include *Every Breath* (HighTide Festival Theatre); *The Wonderful Discovery of Witches* (Dawn State Theatre Company) and *Falling* (Theatre Alibi). Film roles include Saoirse in *Dust* (Average Pig). Amy is delighted to be making her Lyric Theatre debut in *Three Sisters*.

Shin-Fei Chen | *Siu Jing*

Shin-Fei Chen trained at the Royal Welsh College of Music and Drama. Her theatre credits include *Anon* (Welsh National Opera), *In the Beginning Was the End* (dreamthinkspeak), and *Avenue Q* (Upstairs at the Gatehouse). Her screen credits include *Doctor Who* (BBC), *The 101-Year-Old Man Who Skipped Out on the Bill and Disappeared* (FLX), and *Jason Bourne* (Universal). This is her first Lyric Theatre Belfast production.

Christine Clare | *Marianne*

Christine trained at Manchester Metropolitan. Lyric Theatre credits: *Fast and Loose*. Other theatre credits: *East Belfast Girl* (Ballymac Friendship Centre); *Moving On* (The Black Box); *Playground* (Down Arts Centre); *Wings* and *A Million Things* (Contact Theatre); *Meanwhile* (Octagon Theatre); *In Pursuit of Oblivion* (Hebden Bridge/Darwin Library Theatre); *JB Shorts 6, 7 & 9* (Joshua Brooks); *Future*

Shock (The Lowry); *Pawn* (Octagon Theatre/Oldham Coliseum/Southwark Playhouse). Film and TV credits: *Coronation Street* (ITV); *Bedlam* (Red Production Company); *Fuel* (Josh Brogan Productions); *You Bring Something Back* (ITV Fixers); *Timeline* (Neon Creative Studios). Christine is the honoured winner of the 2009 Alan Bates Award, chosen by the Actors Centre to be given to a graduate who they consider to be an 'Outstanding Actor'. Christine was also nominated for the 2009 Best Fringe Performance M.E.N Theatre Awards.

Niall Cusack | *Beattie*

Niall has forty years' experience working on stage, and in radio, films and television. Credits at the Lyric Theatre include *Here Comes the Night, Mother Courage, Philadelphia, Here I Come!, Dancing at Lughnasa, Translations, The Taming of the Shrew, Pygmalion, Oliver Twist, Observe the Sons of Ulster Marching Towards the Somme, The Crucible, A Life, Round the Big Clock, Noises Off, On McQuillan's Hill, Brothers of the Brush.* Other theatre credits include *Henry and Harriet* (Kabosh); *Playboy of the Western World, Aladdin, Dangerous Obsession, Arsenic and Old Lace, All Souls Night* (all Arts Theatre); *Pinocchio, The Importance of Being Earnest, The Wizard of Oz, The Wind in the Willows* (all Riverside Theatre); *The Merchant of Venice, Endgame* (Belfast Actors Cooperative); *Scenes from the Big Picture* (Prime Cut). Television credits include *Scapegoat, Betrayal of Trust, 37 Days, Line of Duty* (all BBC); *Game of Thrones* (HBO); *Wodehouse in Exile* (Great Meadow Productions). Film credits include *The Railway Station Man* (BBC Films) and *Good Vibrations* (Canderblinks).

Matthew Forsythe | *Rod*

Matthew Forsythe was born in Lisburn, and trained at Drama Studio London. Theatre credits include: *Mydidae* (Prime Cuts Productions); *Our Boys* (Duchess Theatre, London); *Damage* (Outburst Festival, Belfast); *Cabaret* (The MAC, Belfast); Little Red Riding Hood (Waterfront and Armagh); *Chekhov Vaudevilles* (Brockley Jack); *Sense and Sensibility* (Rosemary Branch/tour, London); *Opening Ceremony, Henry the Fifth* (New Royal Shakespeare Theatre /Swan Theatre, Stratford); *Hang of the Gaol* (Brockley Jack Theatre); *Small Family Business* (Camden People's Theatre, London); *My Night with Reg* (Grange Court, London). TV credits include: *The Fall* (BBC); *My Mother and Other Strangers* (BBC); *Chalk and Cheese* (Joyce Greenaway); *Grace* (Rivendall Films); *Tolerance* (Magnus Ahlberg); *Just Keep Floating* (Josh Harris Films).

Gerard Jordan | *Teddy*

Theatre credits include: *'Em 2 Balloons* (Balloon Factory); *Mistletoe and Crime, Mixed Marriage, Shadow of a Gunman, American Buffalo* (Lyric Theatre); *The Sweetie Bottle, Fishers of Men* (Brassneck Theatre); *Both Sides: Static/Yes So I Said Yes* (Ransom Productions); *The West Awakes* (Kabosh); *Scenes from the Big Picture* (Prime Cut/National Theatre London); *Don Carlos, The Bonefire* (Rough Magic); *The Force of Change* (Royal Court); *The Laughter of Our Children* (Dubblejoint Theatre Co.). Screen credits include: *Shooting for Socrates* (New Black Films); *71* (Wrap Films); *Foyles War* (ITV); *The Fall, Five Minutes of Heaven, Pulling Moves, Divorcing Jack, As the Beast Sleeps, Give My Head Peace* (BBC); *Game of Thrones* (HBO); *Fifty Dead Men Walking* (Brightlight Pictures); *Savage* (SP Films), *Peacefire* (Mayfly Entertainment); *Accelerator* (Gazboro Films); *Boxed* (Fireproof Films); *Gun* (Raw Nerve Productions).

Lewis MacKinnon | *Baron*

Lewis trained at the Oxford School of Drama and with the National Youth Theatre. His work in theatre includes *Not That Kind of Guy* (Paines Plough Roundabout); *Your Last Breath* (Southwark Playhouse); *Black Sheep* (Soho Theatre); and *Live Lunch : Kid A Kidder* (Royal Court). Television includes *Doctors* (BBC). Film includes *Dragonheart : Dragonborn* (Universal Films); *The Wyrd* (The Raging Quiet); and *Chosen* (Sterling Pictures).

Julie Maxwell | *Orla*

Previous Lyric shows include *Joseph and His Technicolour Dream Coat, Be My Baby, The Miser and The Crucible*. Other work includes *Bebo and Diablo* (Edinburgh Fringe); *Flesh Dense, Tracy Plot, Cleaners* (OMAC); *Hostel* (Grand Opera House); *Love, New Kid* (Replay NI Tour); *Lanciatore* (Belfast Circus School); *Poor Cousin* (Hampstead Theatre); *Widows* (Sherman Theatre); *Case of the Frightened Lady, The Government Inspector, Oh What a Lovely War* (Bruiser NI tour); *Slimmer for Christmas, My Big Fat Belfast Christmas* (Theatre at the Mill); *Mydidae* (The MAC); *The Good Room* (Culturlan). Julie appeared in BBC NI comedy sketch show *Sketchy* series 1 & 2. She received the Kenneth Branagh Renaissance Award 2004 and recently the Arts Council of Northern Ireland Individual Artist Award 2016. She has just finished writing her third play, *Last Orders, at* the Rough Diamond going into production at Theatre at the Mill, Christmas 2016.

Patrick McBrearty | *DJ Cool*

Born in County Donegal, currently Living in Belfast. Graduated from the Royal Central School of Speech and Drama in 2013. Theatre credits include: *Blackout* (Lyric Theatre); *What We Are Made Of* (TinderBox); *After the End* (Pintsize NI); *Under The Hawthorn Tree* (Cahoots NI); *The Tempest* (Terra Nova); *Blinkered* (Sole Purpose); national tour of *Frank Pig Says Hello* (An Grianan Productions); *The Importance of Being Ernest* (Wilde Festival); *Lovers* (Friel Festival). Film credits: *Lost City of Z* (Plan B); *Still Waters* (Carnaby Productions); Web series: *Heads & Tails* (Red Hen).

Julian Moore-Cook | *Simon*

Julian trained at East 15 Drama School in London. Since graduating he has enjoyed working in television, theatre and film. He works as a stand-up comedian and has performed at Edinburgh Fringe Festival. He is currently working and writing for sketch comedy company Shame Aloha. Theatre credits include: *The Rolling Stone* (Orange Tree Theatre); *Twelfth Night* (Iris Theatre); *Our American Cousin* (Finborough Theatre); *Beggar's Opera* (Regents Park Open Air Theatre); *Cleopatra* (Kings Head Theatre); *Wind in the Willows* (Brockwell Park); *The Education of Adolf Hitler* (Tristan Bates Theatre). Television and film includes: *24 Live Another Day*, *Casualty*, and *Mission Impossible: Ghost Protocol*.

Aidan O'Neill | *Andy*

Aidan is from Coalisland in Tyrone but has lived in London for a number of years. Credits include *The Non-Stop Connolly Show* (Finborough); *Dancing Shoes: The George Best Story* (Grand Opera House Belfast/UK tour); *Stones in His Pockets* (UK our); *Best of Friends* (The Landor); *A Dream Across the Ocean* (Ashcroft, Croydon); *Grimes and McKees' Giant Christmas Journey* (Grand Opera House Belfast); *Women on the Verge of HRT* (UK tour); *Dance Hall Days* (RiversideStudios); *A Midsummer Night's Dream* (Ludlow Shakespeare Festival); *Mays Panto Party* (BBC1). Aidan has appeared in panto at the Grand Opera House, Belfast, for six seasons, also at the Liverpool Empire and His Majesty's Theatre, Aberdeen. He is an experienced presenter having presented for Nickelodeon, MTV and Paramount. He is also the sole voice of Irish cartoon *Life Boat Luke* currently being aired on RTE/ABC Australia and Anamaina USA.

Tim Treloar | *Vershinin*

Tim trained at LAMDA. Theatre credits include: *King Charles III* (Sydney Theatre Company); *King Lear* (Chichester and BAM); *Richard II, Romeo and Juliet, Back to Methuselah, Thomas More, Sejanus, Believe What You Will, Heart Of Robin Hood* (RSC); *Macbeth* (West End and Broadway); *Henry V* (National); *Rose Rage* (West End); *Mountain Language* (Royal Court); *Realism, I Kiss Your Heart* (Soho Theatre); *Twelfth Night* (Chichester); *Birdsong* (tour); *Beggar's Opera* (Orange Tree); *Duchess of Malfi, Volpone, Dr Faustus, School for Scandal* (Greenwich Theatre); *Midsummer Night's Dream* (Squerries Court); *Sing Yer Heart Out for the Lads* (tour). TV and film credits: *Dark Heart, Crossing Lines, Father Brown, Mammon, Mayday, Holby City, Liquid Bomb Plot, Doctors, Framed, Silent Witness, Lewis, The Bill, Casualty, Touch of Frost, Bombshell, The Brief, Mine All Mine, Ryse, Single, Foyle's War, Midsomer Murders, The Bench, Bomber, Hundred*

Streets, Maleficent, Crown and the Dragon, Macbeth, Wondrous Oblivion. Tim also has extensive radio experience including plays for BBC Radio, and is The Third Doctor Who for Big Finish Productions.

Lucy Caldwell | *Writer*

Lucy Caldwell was born in Belfast in 1981. She is the author of several stage plays, including *Leaves, Guardians* and *Notes to Future Self*, and numerous radio dramas, as well as three novels and a collection of short stories. Awards include the Rooney Prize for Irish Literature, the Dylan Thomas Prize, the George Devine Award for Most Promising Playwright, the Susan Smith Blackburn Award, the Imison Award, a Fiction Uncovered Award and a Major Individual Artist Award from the Arts Council of Northern Ireland. She was shortlisted for the 2012 BBC International Short Story Award and won the Commonwealth Writers' Award (Canada and Europe) in 2014. Her website is **www.lucycaldwell.com**

Selina Cartmell | *Director*

Selina is Artistic Director of the multi-award winning Siren Productions and the recipient of three Irish Times Theatre Awards for Best Director. Her work for Siren Productions includes: *Fando and Lis, La Musica, Titus Andronicus* (four Irish Times Theatre Awards including Best Production), *Shutter, Macbeth, Medea* (nominated for five Irish Times Theatre Awards), *The Lulu House, The Making of 'Tis Pity She's A Whore, A Tender Thing, Grounded.* Other work includes: *Catastrophe* (also Barbican), *Festen, Sweeney Todd* (Gate Theatre, Best Opera Production, Irish Times Theatre Awards); *By the Bog of Cats, King Lear, Woman and Scarecrow, Only an Apple, Big Love* (Abbey Theatre); *Rigoletto* (OTC); *Punk Rock* (Lyric Theatre, nominated for six Irish Times Theatre Awards); *Override* (Watford Palace, London); *The Broken Heart* (TFANA, New York, Lucille Lortel Award); *The Cordelia Dream* (Royal Shakespeare Company); *The Prince and the Pauper* (Unicorn Theatre, London); *The Giant Blue Hand* (Ark Theatre); *Molly Sweeney* (Leicester Curve); *Here Lies, Passades* (Operating Theatre). Selina was mentored by world-renowned director Julie Taymor under the Rolex Mentor and Protégé Arts Initiative.

Alex Lowde | *Set and Costume Designer*

Opera includes: *Rigoletto* (Opera Theatre Company Wexford, UK tour); *The Adventures of Mr Broucek* (Opera North and Scottish Opera); *Tobias and the Angel* (Young Vic); *The Lion's Face*, *The Nose* (ROH2/The Opera Group); *Paradise Moscow* (Royal Academy of Music); *The Gentle Giant* (ROH Education); *Le Nozze di Figaro* (Sadler's Wells). Theatre includes: *Dedication* (Nuffield Theatre, Southampton); *Dutchman* (Young Vic); *Linda* (Royal Court); *Lines* (The Yard); Miss Julie (Aarhus Theatre); *Game* (Almeida); *Stink Foot* (The Yard); *'Tis Pity She's a Whore* (Shakespeare's Globe); *Krapp's Last Tape* (Sheffield Theatre); *Enjoy* (West Yorkshire Playhouse); *The Body of an American* (Gate); *Edward II* (National Theatre); *A Christmas Carol, Takin' over the Asylum, The Marriage of Figaro* (Edinburgh Lyceum); *Innocence* (Scottish Dance Theatre); *Carousel* (Royal Conservatoire of Scotland); *Blake Diptych* (Laban); *Victoria Station/One for the Road* (Young Vic/Print Room); *A Clockwork Orange* (Stratford East); *While You Lie* (Traverse); *The Glass Menagerie, Anna Karenina, Beauty and the Beast, She Town, A Doll's House, The Elephant Man, Equus* (Dundee Rep).

Ciaran Bagnall | *Lighting Designer*

Lyric Theatre lighting designs: *St Joan, Pentecost* (winner of Irish Times Theatre Award, Best Lighting Design), *Philadephia, Here I Come!, The Little Prince* and *Pump Girl*. Lighting and set design: *White Star of the North*. Recent lighting designs include: *On Corporation Street, Angel Meadow* (HOME, Manchester); *The Pillowman* (Gaiety); *A Taste of Honey* (Hull Truck); *Much Ado about Nothing* (RSC/Noël Coward Theatre); *Macbeth, Wizard of Oz, Sweeney Todd, Romeo and Juliet* (Octagon Theatre, Bolton). Recent lighting and set designs include: *Macbeth* (Shakespeare's Globe); *Singin' in the Rain* (UK tour); *Sleeping Beauty* (Hull Truck); *Scorch, The God of Carnage, Lally the Scut, Planet Belfast, Tejas Verdes, I Am My Own Wife* (MAC); *Othello* (RSC); *Two/ Two 2, A View from the Bridge, Love Story, Twelfth Night, Piaf, The Glass Menagerie, Of Mice and Men, Habeas Corpus, Oleanna* (Octagon Theatre, Bolton); *A Slight Ache* and *Landscape* (Lyttelton Theatre, National Theatre).

Isobel Waller-Bridge | *Composer and Sound Designer*

Theatre includes: *Seven Acts of Mercy, Hecuba* (RSC); *The Philanderer* (Orange Tree); *Dutchman* (Young Vic); *The End of Longing* (West End); *The Damned United* (West Yorkshire Playhouse); *Kite* (International Mime Festival); *By the Bog of Cats* (Abbey Theatre); *Forever Yours Mary Lou, The One That Got Away, Exit the King* (Ustinov); *The Hook* (Royal & Derngate); *Hope Place* (Liverpool Everyman); *King Lear* (Chichester Festival Theatre/BAM); *Neville's Island* (Chichester Festival Theatre/West End); *If Only* (Minerva Theatre); *Billy Liar, Orlando, So Here We Are* (Manchester Royal Exchange); *Posh* (Nottingham Playhouse/Salisbury); *Uncle Vanya* (St James Theatre); *Incognito* (Bush Theatre, Off West End Award for Best Sound Design); *Not the Worst Place* (Sherman Cymru); *Yellow Face* (National Theatre); *Lampedusa, Fleabag, The Girl with the Iron Claws, Blink* (Soho Theatre); Ideal World Season (Watford Place Theatre); *Forever House* (Theatre Royal Plymouth); *Sleuth* (Watermill); *Mydidae* (Traverse Theatre/West End); *Gruesome Playground Injuries* (Gate Theatre). Film and TV includes: *Fleabag* (BBC/Amazon); additional music for *War and Peace* (BBC/Weinstein Company, Emmy nominated, Best Original Music for a Drama Series); *True Appaloosa* (BBC4); *James* (Winner, Best Composer Underwire Film Festival); *Tracks, The Frozen Planet: Making of* (BBC); *Secret Symphony* (Samsung/The Times); *Gilead* (Radio 3); *Physics* (Winner BFI Best Film Best of Boroughs).

Dylan Quinn | *Movement Director*

Dylan Quinn has been working as a choreographer, dance artist and facilitator for over twenty years. In 2009 he established Dylan Quinn Dance Theatre (DQDT) and has created six company performances as well as several commissioned productions for Maiden Voyage Dance Company, Ludus Dance, Birmingham Dance Exchange and Birmingham Royal Ballet. Dylan has performed across the UK, Ireland and internationally, and recently presented DQDT production *Fulcrum* as part of Dublin Dance Festival 2016, *Commencez!* (Paris Beckett 16/Instances Festival, France). Dylan also performed in *Catastrophe* directed by Adrian Dunbar in Paris 16 and during the Enniskillen Happy Days Festival. His work has been presented regularly at The MAC Belfast and across Ireland. He has worked with a range of actors including Stanley Townsend, Orla Charleton, Frank Mc Cusker and Dan Gordon. Dylan has extensive experience of working within community settings and particularly within a peace and conflict context.

Louisa Sanfey | *Assistant Director*

Louisa Sanfey completed an MFA in Theatre Directing from the Lir Academy in 2014. She recently directed *Breaks* at Tiger Dublin Fringe, developed through the Barbican Guildhall Open Lab. Recent work includes the short plays *Half-Baked* and *Gatecrashing* at Theatre 503's Rapid Write Response Night, and a rehearsed reading of a new play, *New History*, by Gillian Greer at Smock Alley Theatre. Previous credits include *The Bells Of* (Theatre Upstairs), *Trifles* (Granary Theatre), *Foxfinder* (The Lir), *The Walls* (Edinburgh Fringe) and *The Gut Girls* (Bloomsbury Theatre). As an Assistant Director she has worked on *The Walworth Farce* (Landmark Productions, directed by Sean Foley) and *Angel Meadow* (ANU/ HOME Manchester, directed by Louise Lowe). Louisa founded Bez Kinte theatre collective in 2015.

Welcome

Change – resetting, realigning, reimagining – has been a constant theme in the Lyric's programme this year.

We opened our 2016 season with a new adaptation of a modern English classic, Willy Russell's *Educating Rita*, which we transported geographically and vernacularly from Liverpool to Belfast, reminding ourselves in the process of the universality of the desire for self-betterment.

Our production of Bernard Shaw's *St Joan* was carried from its medieval French world of castles and courts to a modern office setting to reflect where social power today resides, while Conor McPherson's new translation of the 1970s German fable *The Nest* produced a story retold for a twenty-first century Anglo-Irish audience.

Lucy Caldwell has gone a step further with her radical new interpretation of Chekhov's masterpiece *Three Sisters*. No longer do we find Olga, Maria and Irina contemplating the meaning of their lives from the confines of a provincial Russian garrison town in the early years of the twentieth century; instead we meet Orla, Marianne and Erin living through the dark days of the Troubles in 1990s Belfast, building uneasy relationships with the British troops stationed in Northern Ireland and cautiously appraising their immigrant, soon-to-be sister-in-law Siu Jing.

It's a coruscating, unashamedly contemporary take on the Russian classic that showcases Lucy Caldwell's talents as a thought-provoking playwright as well as an award-winning author. It also causes us to pause and reflect on the incredible changes that have occurred in Belfast over the past twenty-odd years. And it is this sense of impermanence and mutability that we try to capture day-in, day-out at the Lyric, holding a mirror up to society, to ourselves, to the giants of western literature, and reflecting on our infinite, extraordinary capacity to change.

Jimmy Fay
Executive Producer
September 2016

LYRIC
THEATRE

Staff

Board of Directors
Sir Bruce Robinson (Chairman)
Stephen Douds (Vice Chair)
Phil Cheevers
Nicky Dunn
Henry Elvin
Patricia McBride
Sid McDowell
Dr Mark Phelan

Patron
Liam Neeson OBE

Artist in Residence
Duke Special

Executive Producer
Jimmy Fay

Apprentice Producer
Bronagh McFeely

Chief Operating Officer
Ciaran McAuley

Literary Manager
Rebecca Mairs

Head of Marketing and Communications
Simon Goldrick

Marketing Manager
Aisling McKenna

Marketing Officer
Aiveen Kelly

Company Stage Manager
Kate Miller

Deputy Stage Managers
Tracey Lindsay
Aimee Yates

Assistant Stage Managers
Louise Bryans
Stephen Dix

Production Manager
Alan McCracken

Technical Manager
Keith Ginty

Technicians
Damian Cox
Ian Vennard
Tighearnan O'Neill

Wardrobe Supervisor
Enda Kenny

Wardrobe Assistant
Erin Charteris

Administration Manager
Clare Gault

Administration Assistant
Cat Rice

Head of Finance
Deirdre Ferguson

Finance Manager
Micheal Meegan

Housekeeping
Debbie Duff
Amanda Rchards
Samantha Walker

Head of Creative Learning
Philip Crawford

**Creative Learning
Co-Ordinator**
Niki Doherty

**Creative Learning
Assistant**
Pauline McKay

Creative Learning Intern
Erin Hoey

**Customer Service
Manager**
Ciara McCann

Duty Managers
Rebecca Cooney
Marina Hampton
Barry Leonard
Ashlene McGurk

Maitre D'
Cliff Hylands

Chef
Ross McMullan

Box Office Supervisor
Emily White

**Box Office
Deputy Supervisor**
Paul McCaffrey

**Customer Service and
Box Office Staff**
Pamela Armstrong
Lauren Bailey
Luke Bannon
Michael Bingham
Carla Bryson
Paula Ruth Carson-Lewis
Rebecca Cooney
Hannah Conlon
Emmett Costello
Stephen Coulter
Andrew Cowan
Ellison Craig
Gary Crossan
Alacoque Davey
Catherine Davison
Amanda Doherty
Scott English
Darren Franklin
Catriona Grant
Chris Grant
Adele Gribbon
Peter Hackett
Simon Hall
Laura Hamill
Marina Hampton
David Hanna
Cathal Henry
Teresa Hill
Erin Hoey
Aaron Hughes
Niamh Johnson
Megan Keenan

Gerard Kelly
Julie Lamberton
Helen Lavery
Janette Loughlin
Radek Maclclak
Megan Magill
Colm McAteer
Aoife McCloskey
Collette McEntee
Sarah McErlain
Patricia McGreevy
Ashlene McGurk
Colin McHugh
Mary McManus
Cathan McRoberts
Catherine Moore
Donal Morgan

Edite Muceniece
Seamus O'Hara
Bernadette Owens
Patrick Quinn
Bobbi Rai Purdy
Geraldine Reynolds
Hayley Russell
Michael Shotton
Ciara Ward
Susannah Wilson

Volunteers

Jordyn Cummings
Bernadette Fox
Jennifer Kerr
Jake Kieran
Alana McAlister
Melissa Patty

Lyric Theatre Supporters

Principal funder:

Also funded by: I

 Belfast
City Council

Main Stage sponsor:

 Danske Bank

Corporate Lounge sponsor:

 AbbeyBondLovis

The Lyric Theatre is also generously supported by:

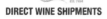 **PHOENIX** NATURAL GAS

 Belfast Harbour

 fona **CAB**

 TEMPLETON ROBINSON

In-Kind Sponsors:

DIRECT WINE SHIPMENTS

 bailies

The Belfast International Arts Festival

As a young man growing up in Belfast in the seventies, I had read all of Chekhov's plays before I had seen any of them on stage. In Three Sisters particularly, the combination of unfulfilled lives lived in a provincial town replete with disappointments and frustrations and belief in a better existence in the sophisticated, cosmopolitan metropolis greatly resonated with my younger self. I was therefore delighted to learn last year that local novelist and playwright, Lucy Caldwell – who had featured in our 2015 festival – was working on a 1990's resetting of Three Sisters in Belfast. We're honored to be able to support her and the production as well as continuing our wonderful relationship with the Lyric Theatre.

There is a sense of uncertainty that pervades throughout Three Sisters that is echoed in the themes and many of the events in this year's festival. For example, the first of our programming themes, Nineteen Sixteen reminds us of the uncertain global outcomes of the Great War and differing perceptions and attitudes to how history is made and viewed. Artists ranging from New York's Taylor Mac through to Colm Tóibín, Olwen Fouéré and Crash Ensemble will be helping us to reflect on notions of authority, class, empire, gender, human rights, patriotism and war in a variety of festival events.

A centerpiece of this year's Festival and featured under our World in Motion theme is the Irish premiere at The Grand Opera House of David Greig's new version of The Suppliant Women by the Greek dramatist, Aeschylus (the world's second oldest play and the first dramatic work to feature the word "democracy") that tells the story of 50 women fleeing war torn North Africa and crossing the Mediterranean for an unsure future in Europe.

To find out more about these and other events in our 2016 programme, simply go to www.belfastinternationalartsfestival.com

Richard Wakely
Director, Ulster Bank Belfast International Arts Festival

Belfast International Arts Festival Supporters

Title Sponsor:

Principal Funders:

LOTTERY FUNDED

of Northern Ireland

tourism
northernireland

BRITISH COUNCIL
Northern Ireland

Department for
Communities
www.communities-ni.gov.uk

Belfast
City Council

Three Sisters

Anton Chekhov (1860–1904), Russian dramatist and short-story writer, was the son of a grocer and the grandson of a serf. After graduating in medicine from Moscow University in 1884, he began to make his name in the theatre with the one-act comedies *The Bear*, *The Proposal* and *The Wedding*. His earliest full-length plays, *Ivanov* (1887) and *The Wood Demon* (1889), were not successful, and *The Seagull* (1896) was a failure until a triumphant revival by the Moscow Art Theatre in 1898. This was followed by *Uncle Vanya* (1899), *Three Sisters* (1901) and *The Cherry Orchard* (1904).

Lucy Caldwell was born in Belfast in 1981. She is the author of several stage plays, including *Leaves*, *Guardians* and *Notes to Future Self*, and radio dramas including *Girl From Mars*, *Avenues of Eternal Peace* and *Dear Baby Mine*, as well as three novels and a collection of short stories. Awards include the Rooney Prize for Irish Literature, the Dylan Thomas Prize, the George Devine Award for Most Promising Playwright, the Susan Smith Blackburn Award, the Imison Award, a Fiction Uncovered Award and a Major Individual Artist Award from the Arts Council of Northern Ireland. She was shortlisted for the 2012 BBC International Short Story Award and won the Commonwealth Writers' Award (Canada and Europe) in 2014.

also by Lucy Caldwell from Faber

LEAVES
NOTES TO FUTURE SELF

ANTON CHEKHOV

Three Sisters

in a version by
LUCY CALDWELL
from a literal translation by Helen Rappaport

FABER & FABER

First published in 2016
by Faber and Faber Limited
74–77 Great Russell Street
London WC1B 3DA

Typeset by Country Setting, Kingsdown, Kent CT14 8ES
Printed in England by CPI Group (UK) Ltd, Croydon, CRO4YY

A CIP record for this book
is available from the British Library

ISBN 978–0–571–33491–9

4 6 8 10 9 7 5

For my sisters, of course

Acknowledgements

I am indebted to Anna Lo, whose story was in my mind as I wrote this version of *Three Sisters*. I would also like to thank Yuen Chau Sze, who shared her stories with me, Yennis Cheung, who helped with the Cantonese phrases, and all those from the Chinese community in Belfast who came to meet with me and share their experiences.

Masha's speech about faith in Act Two has long been one of my favourite speeches in theatre, and it seems apt here to acknowledge those who kept faith in both me and this play, even as mine flickered: Jimmy Fay and all those at the Lyric; Selina Cartmell; Dinah Wood; Simon Trussler; and most of all, Harriet Pennington Legh, every step of this journey to Moscow.

Introduction

There is a certain house you walk past, every now and then, and when you do you dream about what it must be like to live there. Sometimes you make a detour there especially: a certain mood, a slant of light, and for days you think of nothing else, seized by wild, strange hope and a burning conviction that it has to, will, be yours.

Then one day someone gives you a key and says, 'Go inside.'

The structure is sound, carefully planned and built and tested by the years. You don't need to blaze in with bulldozers and start again entirely. But at the same time, too, you need to inhabit it utterly: you need to fill it with everything that's meaningful to you, to let yourself belong to it, or it to you.

You blow away some cobwebs here. You knock a wall through there. You discover, behind some peeling wallpaper, pencilled marks by people long gone, which delight you, and you add yours, too, and carefully stick the curling paper back down. There are stained-glass windows and a beautiful parquet floor and you need do nothing to either but clean and polish them and let the jewelled light fall. You spend a long time sitting in a window seat overlooking the garden, watching the sunlight on the leaves in the wind. A cherry tree is bowing over but still producing fruit and still will, decades from now. The house will be here long after you have gone. You get to work.

I'm far from the first, I know, to use this analogy. But it seems apposite, seemed often, indeed, the only way of imagining the play. I became obsessed with the house at the centre of the play, and all it represents, of and for the characters. I inhabited the house, too, not just metaphorically but as literally as possible: my husband is an architect, and together we drew up plans. This room here, the cellar stairs here. A bay window, a kitchen with a Belfast sink. I traced the movements of my characters through the house, the years, and back again, over and over.

Writing this version of Chekhov's *Three Sisters* felt like coming full circle, coming home, in more ways than one. My own nineties Belfast, my own teenage years. My first major play in my home city, my first play in the theatre I first saw plays in. I came back, too, to the lines of poetry Blu-tacked to my wall in various student bedrooms as I was writing my very first novel, my very first anything, lines from Louis MacNeice's poem 'Selva Oscura':

> A house can be haunted by those who were never there
> If there was where they were missed.
> [. . .]
> The haunting anyway is too much.
> You have to leave the house to clear the air.

This is a play of hauntings, yearnings, leavings real and imagined. A play of love, and loss, and letting go. I have left, and I have come back. Or maybe you can never truly leave at all.

Lucy Caldwell
September 2016

Three Sisters in this version was first performed at the Lyric Theatre, Belfast, on 15 October 2016. The cast, in order of appearance, was as follows:

Siu Jing Shin-Fei Chen
Orla Julie Maxwell
Marianne Christine Clare
Erin Amy Blair
Baron Lewis MacKinnon
Beattie Niall Cusack
Simon Julian Moore-Cook
Vershinin Tim Treloar
Andy Aidan O'Neill
DJ Cool Patrick McBrearty
Rod Matthew Forsythe
Teddy Gerard Jordan

Director Selina Cartmell
Set and Costume Designer Alex Lowde
Lighting Designer Ciaran Bagnall
Composer and Sound Designer Isobel Waller-Bridge
Movement Director Dylan Quinn
Vocal Coach Brendan Gunn
Assistant Director Louisa Sanfey
Literal Translator Helen Rappaport

Characters

Orla

Marianne

Erin

Baron

Beattie

Simon

Vershinin

Andy

DJ Cool

Siu Jing

Teddy

Rod

Setting

Belfast, 1990s

THREE SISTERS

Prologue

Siu Jing. She speaks directly to the audience.

Siu Jing Well, here we are.

Pause.

This is the place I keep coming back to. This is where everything began to change forever.

The house is full of soldiers. They are not there, not really. But they are in every day of my memories. On every corner. In every street. Sometimes they stalk through my dreams.

It is the fifth of May 1993.

Or as I used to think, the fourteenth day of the third lunar month in Gui-Leen (雞年): the Year of the Rooster.

It's a long time since I thought like that. For years now I have dreamed almost entirely in English. You don't realise as it's happening, then one day you realise it happened long ago.

The lights up slightly.

These are my sisters. Well, they're not yet my sisters, but they soon will be.

Here is Orla. Orla is always busy. Orla always complains about how busy she is but, in truth, she is scared that if she stops, she will be forced to confront . . . herself. She buries herself in being a mother, or as close to a mother-figure as they've had for a long time.

This is Marianne. Nobody understands Marianne, herself least of all. Right now, she is thinking that she wants to die. Or that maybe she doesn't want to die, but she doesn't want to live any more. Not like this. This – here, now – this isn't life. This day, and all the days to come. The thought of them paralyses her. If something doesn't happen, soon, she is going to kill herself. That's what she's thinking.

And this is Erin. Erin is the baby – the joker – the flibbertigibbet. That's what her father used to call her – his flibbertigibbet. She was the only one that knew how to make him smile. This is still her role – until the day she decides she doesn't want to play it any more, at all.

It's Erin's eighteenth birthday. It is also the first anniversary of their father's death, but the sisters are determined to celebrate anyway.

I am nineteen – just one year older than Erin.

So.

These are my sisters and this is their story.

It is also my story. It might not have my name on it, but it is my story too.

And this is where it begins. An evening in May.

The lights up fully.
Siu Jing watches the sisters.
She leaves.

Act One

Belfast, 1993.
  May. Early evening. Blue skies.
  Orla, Marianne and Erin.
  It is Erin's eighteenth birthday and the sisters are getting ready for her party. It is fancy dress. Erin is dressed as Supergirl and Orla is Marge Simpson.
  The radio is playing Kylie Minogue's 'I Should Be So Lucky'.

DJ Cool Now folks, regular listeners will know that it's extremely unusual for me to interrupt the *Non-Stop Drive-Time Hour* but this is a very special occasion. Today, the fifth of May, is not just any day: and so a special shout-out to the lovely Erin who turns eighteen today! Forget the fourth, May the fifth be with you! D'you like what I did there? Do you? Do you get it? May the fifth –

  Marianne turns the radio abruptly off.

Erin Hey! That was my shout-out!

Marianne I swear, I can't take another second of him.

Orla Come on, girls. Here we are. The fifth of May. We've done it.
  How's it been a whole year already?
  Do you remember how cold it was? We were foundered. I mean it was absolutely Baltic. Here, what do you reckon people actually from the Baltic say when it gets cold?

  Pause.

D'you remember when they took the coffin away, God. It was lashing it down, absolutely lashing it. Your man playing the Last Post to us and the gravestones. Why d'you reckon no one came, was it 'cause he was Catholic or 'cause he was English?

Erin Why are you doing this?

Baron, Beattie and Simon are outside. Baron and Beattie are smoking.

Orla 'On May nights, when so many doors are closed, there is one that is barely ajar.' Where's that from? I can't remember where that's from. It's been going round my head all day. Oh God Almighty, I want to get away from here!

Beattie Away and jump!

Baron You are talking bollocks.

Marianne starts singing 'I Should Be So Lucky'.

Orla Stop it. Marianne! You're doing my head in.

All afternoon all evening and every single weekend, hearing yet another bunch of stuck-up kids who don't give a shit sawing their way through scales that they obviously haven't bothered practising since the last lesson – is it any wonder I have a permanent headache? It's almost literally boring me to death. The only thing that's keeping me going –

Erin Is America.

She raps the first few lines of 'Fresh Prince of Bel-Air'.

We should just do it you know. Put this house on the market and get on a plane.

Orla Yes! D'you know I don't even care where we go. New York, California, Philadelphia, Bel-Air –

Erin Well, there's no way Andy will stay here once his thesis is done. The only thing stopping us is her.

Orla She can get a J-1 and come for the summer.

Marianne (*sings, to the tune of 'I Should Be So Lucky'*) 'I should be so lucky, with my rubber ducky, strangle Mrs Mangle too . . .'

Erin See? Sorted.

Orla Someone got up on the right side of bed this morning.

Erin D'you know I just woke up and thought: it's my birthday! And for once the sun was shining and I suddenly thought of Mum, and when we were kids, and it was like the sunshine was this message from her, like – anything is possible?

Orla You're shining with it. And you, Marianne, you always look well in yourself. And Andy would if only he'd lose some weight. God, I hate to say it but he's piling on the pounds and it does nothing for him. But who am I to talk, you'd think I was forty I look that haggard. But no you're right – here we are, I mean we've made it through a whole year – the sun is shining and for once my headache's gone. And you have to remember: everything that happens, happens for a reason.

Pause.

And one of these days I'll meet the love of my life.

Baron I'm sorry, but that's complete and utter bollocks. (*Calling in.*) Can we come in yet?

Erin No. Hang on.

The sisters put the finishing touches to their costumes.

OK. Yous can come in. Ta-daa!

Baron, Beattie and Simon enter.

Beattie Ach will you look at you.

Erin Do you like it?

Baron You look beautiful, Erin.

Erin Who are you meant to be?

Baron Who am I meant to be? Can you not tell?

Simon Fail, mate. Epic fail.

Baron 'This is the final cruise of the Starship Enterprise under my command, boldly going where no man . . . where no one has gone before.' I thought you'd appreciate that, Erin.

Simon No girl in the history of girls has ever been turned on by *Star Trek*.

Baron Shut up, Simon.

Marianne That, for the record, is sexist.

Simon Whatever, goth-girl. You haven't made much of an effort, have you?

Marianne I don't do fancy dress.

Erin She needs to get over herself! And here, why aren't you in fancy dress?

Beattie Oh, I'm too old for that sort of stuff-and-nonsense.

Erin Uncle Beattie!

Orla We've got a bag of stuff here. You can have a mask.

Erin And who are you?

Simon Oh, this isn't my costume. You want to see my costume?

Baron Are you actually going to take that coat off now? He's had it on all afternoon. All the way here.

Simon Get ready . . .

Simon starts to unbutton his overcoat.
 Beattie sings the first few lines of 'Button Up Your Overcoat'.

Simon What the fuck is that, man?

Beattie That, son, is before your time.

Simon Well enough of the soundtrack, OK, are you ready?

He whips off his overcoat. He's wearing his full army combat gear.

Baron What are you doing, man? Are you fucking insane?

Simon I don't need no superhero costume. So I've come as . . . myself.

Baron If anyone saw you . . . You could've got yourself killed. You could've got us both killed.

Simon Not scared of anyone, mate. Bring it on.

Erin You've come as yourself?

Simon I know you like a man in uniform.

Baron You are insane.

Simon Take a chill pill, Spock.

Baron I'm not Spock, I'm Captain Kirk.

Simon So court-martial me, Captain Kirk. Sir.

Baron Whatever. Happy birthday, Erin.

Orla Yes, happy birthday, Erin. Now who wants a drink?

Beattie Yes please.

Orla Not you.

Erin Me!

Baron I forgot to say! There's this new honcho at the barracks, some kind of special adviser, ex-military, says he knew your father. Said he'd stop by this evening, if that's alright, pay his respects.

He picks up an acoustic guitar and starts strumming.

Erin Is he old?

Baron Not particularly. I'd say he's . . . fifty?

He strums the guitar.

Erin Oh God. That's ancient. What's he like?

Baron Seems OK. Talks an awful lot though. His wife. His mother-in-law. His two little girls. The fact that his wife's actually his second wife. Oh, and did I mention he talks about his wife and his two little girls?

He sings the opening lines of Teenage Fanclub, 'What You Do to Me'.

She's a complete psycho, apparently. Waltzes around like she's walked off *Little House on the Prairie*, these big long shapeless things and her hair in plaits, and bangs on about 'the male gaze'. And she's always threatening to top herself, just to wind him up. Christ, if it was me I'd have run a mile, but he stays and feels sorry for himself.

Beattie (*reading his newspaper*) Here's one for you, son. They reckon they've got a new cure for baldness.

Simon Fuck off.

Beattie Says here they take the individual hair-follicles from your chest and graft them one by one –

Simon I'll graft you if you don't put a sock in it.

Erin (*to Simon*) You leave him be. (*To Beattie.*) Here, Uncle Beattie!

Beattie Yes, wee pet?

Erin Why do I feel so happy today? It's like – I'm flying. Flying through a high, blue sky, and not a cloud in sight . . .

Beattie You're a wee sunbeam so you are.

Erin As soon as I woke up it was all so clear – like someone had blown the cobwebs away – today is the start of the rest of your life. I don't know what it is I'm going to do but I'm going to do something. I'm going to be someone. I am! I'm sick of just being me. I'm going to be someone else. Someone better. I'm going to make a difference. I'm being serious!

Beattie I know you are, wee pet.

Orla Dad had us up at the skrake of dawn each day, as if we were in the cadets. Erin still wakes up first thing, but then she lies in bed for hours having epiphanies. Look at her. She's deadly serious.

Erin Am I not allowed to be serious? You have to stop treating me like a wee girl, Orla.

Baron I hear you, Erin. You know the way I grew up in The Braids –

Erin We know.

Baron In 'one of the finest examples of Georgian architecture in the city' my mother always used to say.

Such a cold and stuck-up place. See my family – there's not one of them would give you the steam off their piss if you were on fire. I remember my mother sacked the housekeeper once for daring to tell me off. I'd tramped mud all through the house and when she asked me to take off my boots I chucked them at her. Can you believe it? They thought Sandhurst was a fad, my family – they didn't think I'd last a week. But they were wrong! People can change. People can start again. Just look at this place. A year ago – six months ago – who'd've believed it?

Beattie Not me, son.

Baron You don't count.

Simon He's talking about the new generation, mate. You – you're basically wormfood. How much do you smoke? Forty a day? You'll have a massive stroke one of these days – wormfood. If I don't snap first and put a bullet in your brain.

Simon spritzes himself with Cool Water fragrance.

Beattie Well, at least I'll be of use to the worms.

The doorbell goes.

Oh-ho! That'll be for me. I won't be a minute. (*To Erin.*) Don't you move a muscle!

Erin What's he at?

Baron I'd say . . . maybe . . . he's got a certain someone . . . a birthday present.

Erin Oh God, do you think so?

Orla It's always something totally dodgy.

Marianne sings the opening lines of The Velvet Underground, 'Pale Blue Eyes' .

Orla What's up with you?

Marianne sings.
She gets up suddenly.

Where are you off to?

Marianne 'Home'.

Erin Marianne!

Baron It's Erin's birthday, you can't just leave.

Marianne Whatever . . . I'm sorry, hun, you don't want me bringing you down. I'll come back later. I just need to –

Erin Why does everything always have to be about you? The earth doesn't revolve around you, you know.

Orla (*to Marianne*) On you go then. What are you waiting for? I'd swan off if I could. Unfortunately someone needs to stay here and keep things going.

Erin Wise up, you two!

Simon What's the difference between a pussy and a cunt? A pussy's warm and soft, a cunt's what owns it.

Marianne You are a fucking disgrace, you know that?

Simon Takes one to know one!

Marianne (*to Orla*) And you, stop being such a fucking martyr.

Orla Seriously. I'm this close. I'm warning you.

She leaves.
Beattie comes in with a box and unpacks a set of Tyrone crystal: a decanter and goblets.

Erin Oh my God.

Baron I told you . . .

Marianne What the fuck is he thinking? It's her birthday, not her wedding day.

Beattie My wee pets, the three of yous are all I have in the world. I remember, Erin, when you were just a few weeks old. I didn't want to hold you for fear I'd break you. When your mother, God rest her, put this wee scrap of a thing in my arms I couldn't even breathe. 'Don't,' says I. 'You'll be grand,' says she. Oh, it could have been yesterday.

Erin You really shouldn't have.

Beattie Ach get away with you.

Erin No but I mean – seriously. It's too much.

Beattie Too much! Nothing's too much for my wee Erin on her eighteenth birthday. Besides, I got it at a good price: a friend did me a deal.

Marianne And did this friend of yours get it off the back of a lorry?

Beattie What are you implying?

Erin No offence, Uncle Beattie, but what am I supposed to do with a crystal whatchamacallit?

Beattie Well, I shall take it away this minute, then.

Vershinin enters.

Vershinin Ding-dong, ding-dong . . . The front door was open – you want to watch that. Well!

Baron Here he is – it's Vershinin! Sir.

Vershinin Oh, we're among friends, no standing on rank here. At ease. What have we here?

Simon is rapidly putting on his greatcoat.

Erin I thought you said you weren't scared.

Simon I'm not scared but I'm not stupid either.

Baron It's Erin's birthday, Sir.

Vershinin It is? Happy birthday, Erin! Call me Alexander. How do you do. Oh, it is so good finally to be here. Look at you! Aren't you just a sight for sore eyes! So grown up. But surely there are three of you – I remember three little girls. I don't remember your faces but I remember there were three of you. All lined up and in your party dresses.

Erin What were we doing lined up in party dresses?

Vershinin One of you had the nuts, one the potato chips, and the littlest one the napkins. New Year's Eve – 1980, it would have been.

Erin So you knew Daddy?

Vershinin Yes I did. I met your father when I was seconded to the UN in Holland – or was it Germany?

Erin Your accent – where are you from?

Vershinin Well, my parents were Lithuanian Jews who fled in the forties. I was born and raised in the States but life in the UN has taken me all over. Do you know, I think your face is a little familiar.

Marianne Yours isn't.

Erin Orla! Lala, come here, you'll never guess what. Alexander here's from America!

Orla enters.

Vershinin Aha – you must be Orla, the eldest. That makes you Marianne – and you're Erin, the baby. Orla, Marianne and Erin. Erin, Orla, and Marianne.

Orla Whereabouts in America?

Vershinin New York – but it's a long time since I've been back. In fact I've spent more of my life in Europe than I have in the States. It was Germany I first met your father. That's right. I can't believe he's passed away a whole year now. I remember that New Year's Eve as if it was yesterday.

Erin It's a sign, Lala.

Orla We're thinking of moving to America.

Erin Thinking? We're going to be there by the autumn. By the 'fall'. You see? We're practically American already.

Marianne Oh my God! Lala, remember in Germany the one they all called Romeo. It was you! You were Romeo.

Vershinin Guilty as charged.

Marianne Oh my God. I can't believe that was you.

Vershinin Yes, 'Romeo' was a young man. Young, idealistic and desperately in love. I'm afraid all that's fallen by the wayside.

Orla Don't be silly, you're not that old. You've got a better head of hair on you than him. (*Simon.*)

Simon Sign of testosterone, love.

Vershinin All the same, I'm almost fifty now. Fifty! And it's taken me this long to come and see you again, and now you're all grown up.

Erin Mimi, why are you crying?

Marianne I'm not crying.

Erin If you don't stop now you'll set us all off.

Marianne I'm sorry. I just –

Pause.

Vershinin This is a beautiful part of the world, you know. I wasn't expecting it to be so beautiful.

Orla We can't stand it here. The sky is grey and the streets are grey and it rains almost constantly.

Vershinin Oh, but everything is green, so green, and the air so soft and fresh! And only ten minutes' drive from the city centre, you could be in another place entirely.

Simon (*aside*) I fucking hate it. Off the chopper – what the fuck is this place? Fucking damp – fucking miserable. Field after cunting field then when you get to the city it's all been bombed to fuck. Eyes everywhere. Even in the fucking fields there are eyes.

Pause.

Orla I think I do remember you. I remember you talking to Mum.

Beattie God rest her soul.

Vershinin Yes, I knew your mother.

Orla Dad moved us all back here after Mum died 'cause he thought it's what she would have wanted. Gave up the army – joined the RUC – turned everything upside down so we could be here. But she wouldn't have wanted us growing up here. It's the last thing she wanted. She'd hate the fact that she's buried here.

Erin She always said she wanted to be cremated – and her ashes scattered from the Golden Gate Bridge.

Orla She spent a summer in San Francisco once. We've a picture of her with flowers in her hair.

Marianne I can only remember her from photos. I don't remember her face any more, not really. They say you're never truly dead in the hearts of those that loved you. Fuck that. What use is love if it barely lasts a decade after someone's death? It's pointless, all of it, just pointless.

Vershinin Yes. And maybe that's the point of it all.

Marianne Oh, don't give us the time-will-heal bullshit.

Vershinin On the contrary. Time doesn't heal. It just rolls blindly on. And there's nothing we can do about it. We burn brightly for a day, an hour, a moment, and then we're gone, the way of all things. Even the things that seem so important now – the things that seem a matter of life or death – one day they'll be but a footnote in a history book.

Pause.

Isn't it funny to think we have no way of knowing – whatsoever – what, if anything, will matter in the future. Take the Wright brothers. No one believed they could do it. No one would back them – no one would even turn up to watch them. Within twenty years, aviation was a booming industry. Or some crackpot quantum physicist in a bunker somewhere right this instant, trying to convince his colleagues that time travel is possible. Everything we take for granted may yet be overturned. How can they have lived like that? the people of the future will say, and they'll pity us, how naïve and foolish we were, and they'll ridicule and maybe even despise us, too.

Baron Who knows? Maybe they'll envy us. Maybe they'll look back and think: that was a golden age. The ceasefire, for a start – against all the odds, we achieved it. We bloody did it.

Simon Is that the 'royal we', mate?

Baron Piss off – I'm talking.

Simon You're talking out your arse. It's what they teach you in Gordonstoun, is it?

Baron What I mean is – I know there's still a long way to go. I know it's not just happy-ever-after from here on in – but when you think about –

Vershinin I take your point.

Beattie You just said that one day, people will envy us. A wee auld man, acting the maggot. D'you see much to envy about me?

The sound of an electric guitar, playing the Pixies, 'Where Is My Mind?'

Marianne That's our brother Andy.

Erin He's dead clever, Andy. Brain the size of Britain. He's doing his PhD on semi— on semi-something – I couldn't even tell you. Daddy was such an action man, but Andy lives in his head.

Orla We've been taking the mickey all day. He's obsessed with this girl.

Erin Who works in the chinky. She'll be up here for dinner, wait till you see her.

Marianne Over-the-knee socks, hair in pigtails, she has that whole schoolgirl thing going on. He can't be serious about her.

Erin Well, he's been going into the Golden Dragon for takeaway every night for weeks. If he's not careful he's going to turn into a crispy duck.

The music plays.

(*Calling.*) Here, Andy? C'mere, will you? Just for a sec. Andy!

The music stops.
   Andy enters. He is fat and wearing an Akira T-shirt.

Orla This is our brother, Andy.

Vershinin Vershinin.

Andy wipes the sweat from his hand and shakes hands.

Andy Andrew.

Orla Alexander was a friend of Dad's.

Erin And he's from America.

Andy Commiserations, my friend. Henceforth, not a moment's peace shall be yours.

Vershinin Oh, I'm sure they've had enough of me already.

Erin Look what Andy made me for my birthday. (*It is a Coke-can figurine.*)

Vershinin Yes . . . Will you look at that.

Erin And he made that one, too. He gives them all names, makes up stories for them – when we were little he used to make up these huge entire worlds with dragons and warlocks and –

Andy leaves.
   Marianne and Erin take an arm each and drag him back into the room. He protests.

Orla Andy! He doesn't mean to be rude, he's just shy. Andy! Get yourself back over here!

Erin Andy-pandy pudding-and-pie!

Andy Leave me alone.

Marianne He's still annoyed with us. Andy, Alexander used to be called Romeo and he never complained.

Vershinin I took it as a compliment.

Erin Andy-pandy pudding and pie, kissed the girls and made them cry!

Marianne Or should we say kissed *one* girl in particular?

Orla Oh, he's taking a beamer, girls.

Erin Andy's in luuurrve.

Beattie comes up behind Andy and embraces him, sings the first few lines of Right Said Fred, 'I'm Too Sexy', tries to make him dance.

Andy Alright, alright, you're all very funny, you've had your fun. (*Wipes his face.*) I didn't sleep at all last night. I don't feel right. I lay awake reading till four and then I tried to get to sleep but nothing happened. My mind just wouldn't switch off. And then it was morning. It gets light so early these days. I should be making the most of it. I plan to translate a book from Finnish this summer.

Vershinin You read Finnish?

Andy Not yet, but I intend to. Tolkien particularly loved Finnish. It shouldn't be too hard, I read Anglo-Saxon and Old Norse. Besides French and German, of course. Erin here knows some Arabic too, Dad taught her. That's what comes from being an Army brat. It sounds silly, I know, but since Dad died, I've doubled in size. It's as if – he kept us all on such a tight leash. I mean, we're conversant in several languages between us, but dare we actually say anything?

Marianne 'Whatever you say, say nothing.' Oh I hate this place! You always have to watch what you're saying and who you might be talking to and who might be listening and how you pronounce your consonants and what might be betraying you without your even knowing. What's the point of French or German or Finnish or any other language when the only question that matters is are you one of us or one of them? And we're neither – English Catholic Dad and Ulster Protestant Mum, who gave us Irish-sounding names – I mean how fucked-up is that? We're not one thing nor the other, we're nothing.

Vershinin Oh, you're not nothing, Marianne – take it from me, you're not nothing at all. In fact, quite the opposite. Let's say, for the sake of argument, even if you were the only ones like you in this entire country. Worst case scenario! Little by little – day by day – you're ground down until life has finally chewed you up and spits you out. Even then you won't have lived in vain. Just by living you will have shown that a different sort of life here is possible. And after you will come a few more, a few more, and so on, until in the end, people like you will be in the majority. In two, three hundred years life here will be beautiful. We must believe that. We must hope for it – dream of it – imagine it into being. We must cast off the petty hatreds and bigotries of our parents and grandparents and so on and so back. And you are the vanguard! The trailblazers! And yet you say you're nothing. Never say you're nothing. I'd say you're everything. You're the future.

Marianne Well, I'll stay for dinner at any rate.

Erin I wish we'd taped that . . .

Andy has slipped out.

Baron That's very heartening, Sir, to think that in your experience – even after what you've seen in Bosnia, Croatia, in Kuwait – you really think that people can reconcile their differences and work together to make the earth a better place?

Vershinin Yes. (*Gets up.*) So much life in here, so much colour! Do you know, I feel more at home here already than in any place I've ever lived.

Baron That's what I think. I truly believe that people can change. It doesn't matter who they are or where they come from. They can start again.

Pause.

Vershinin If only you could start your life again – but knowing everything you know now. If your life, right up until this day, this very moment, turned out to be a trial run for the real thing. You'd do everything differently. This very room, this very evening in May – this is where my real life would begin. I have a wife, you see, and two little girls – and my wife's not very well. If I had my life over again, I wouldn't marry –

DJ Cool enters and goes straight up to Erin.

DJ Cool Aaaaand a special shout-out to the lovely Erin who turns eighteen today! Forget the fourth, May the fifth be with you! Did you hear it? And to further mark this milestone –

He hands her a cassette.

– a compilation of my Top Twenty Songs to Get the Party Started. Hi there, hi. (*To Vershinin.*) I don't think we've met – Dave – or should I say – DJ Cool. You won't be familiar with my face but you might just have heard my voice – *Drive Time with DJ Cool? Hotting It Up for the Midnight Hour?* (*Kisses Marianne.*) Hiya, babe.

Erin You gave me this at Christmas.

DJ Cool Did I? Well in that case –

He takes the cassette and goes to give it to Vershinin.

You might as well have it. You never know when you might need to – (*Sings as Madonna.*) 'Get into the groove'.

Vershinin Thank you. (*Gets ready to leave.*) Well, it's great to meet you girls –

Orla You're not leaving already?

Erin Stay for dinner!

Orla Yes, come on, you have to stay for dinner.

Vershinin I don't want to outstay my welcome. Happy birthday, Erin.

Erin You have to stay. We always order too much anyway. It's nothing fancy, just an Indian.

The doorbell goes.

Orla Here it is now.

She leaves.
   Vershinin leaves.

DJ Cool Well, kids, let's get this party pumping! (*To Marianne.*) We can't stay long, babe. People to meet, places to be – I said we'd call in at a leaving drinks. Claire Jenkins the station manager – it was her last day today. They've hired the room above the Hatfield. We're all meant to do a turn at karaoke.

He sings the first few lines from Elton John and Kiki Dee, 'Don't Go Breaking My Heart', holding an invisible mike out to Marianne and singing 'her' part in falsetto.

Marianne I'm not going.

DJ Cool What do you mean, babe?

Marianne We'll discuss it later. (*Angrily.*) Fine, OK, whatever, I'll go, just – stop talking at me.

Marianne leaves.
Pause.

DJ Cool (*sings, looks at his watch, looks at the clock*) Your clock is seven minutes fast, did you know that?

The sound of Andy playing 'Where Is My Mind?'
Orla enters.

Orla Alright, folks, dinner's here! Come on, before it gets cold. Can someone give me a hand here?

DJ Cool Still run ragged, I see, Orla. I know how you feel – I was on the graveyard slot last night, then sitting in for Morning Mike until ten, a few hours' kip, then back in for my own *Drivetime* show.

Everyone is gathering and sitting down.

Ah, Orla. There should be a song named 'Orla'.

Orla Well, it wouldn't be a love song, I'll tell you that for free.

A moment.

Beattie You can't beat a good curry.

Marianne You're not to go getting hammered now.

Beattie I haven't been on the tear in almost two years. A wee couple of beers at a birthday party – you wouldn't grudge me that.

Marianne A wee couple of beers – yeah, right. I'm being serious. (*Angrily.*) A whole fucking night at Claire fucking Jenkins' fucking karaoke whatever.

Baron Don't go. Problem solved.

Beattie He's right, wee pet. Just don't go.

Marianne 'Don't go, don't go' – whatever. Fucking hell.

She walks off. Beattie follows.

Beattie Ach, wee love.

Simon He's a randy old goat, that geezer. Here, what's the difference between a ram and a goat?

Baron Give it a rest, mate.

DJ Cool Bottoms up, kids! Here's to the nights we'll never remember with the friends we'll never forget. Here's to those who've seen us at our best and seen us at our worst and can't tell the difference. And here's to our wives and girlfriends – may they never meet.

Vershinin I need a drink. (*Downs a glass.*)

Erin and Baron remain separate.

Erin Marianne is in such a bad mood. I remember when she won the prize to do work experience at the radio station. She thought he was the coolest thing in town. We all did.

Orla Andy, we're waiting.

Andy I'm coming.

Orla Hurry up.

Baron What are you thinking?

Erin Nothing. I don't like your friend Simon. Psy-cho more like. Why did you bring him?

Baron Do you know what – I actually feel sorry for him – I mean he annoys me too sometimes – but I mostly feel sorry for him. He had a really tough time on his first tour, you know. When he got back home his mum found him one night drunk as a skunk, running down the road kicking hedges and shouting, 'Sniper! Sniper!' Hang on. Don't go just yet. What are you thinking?

Pause.

I'll tell you what I'm thinking. We've got our whole lives ahead of us, you and me.

Erin Don't talk about you and me. There is no you and me.

Baron (*not listening*) We're different from the rest of them. We are, Erin. They're full of talk – but you and me, we're going to change the world. We're going to make a difference. We're going to be someone, just like you said.

Erin Stop quoting my own words back at me. I hate it when you do that.

Baron You are so beautiful, you have no idea.

Erin No I'm not. I'm just a stupid nobody. I don't even know what it is I want to do. Sometimes I think –

She is crying. She wipes her face.

Look what you've made me do. My mascara's going to be all down my face.

Siu Jing enters.

Siu Jing Sang yat fai lok (生日快樂), many happy returns]. So many people, I so shy! ley ho ma (你好嗎). Hi, hi, nice to meet you!

Orla gets up and goes to her.
Siu Jing gives Orla an elaborately wrapped gift.

41

Orla And here's Jenny. Her real name is Siu Jing but none of us can say it so we call her Jenny – don't we?

Siu Jing Many – happy – return. So many people! I so shy!

Orla Don't be silly, it's just a few friends and a takeaway. What did I tell you, folks! Andy must've forget to tell her it was fancy dress!

Siu Jing You no like my dress?

Orla Well no, I just meant – you look the same as you always do.

Siu Jing (*tearfully*) Andy like this dress – I wear it specially.

Andy enters.

Andy Look at you. You look –

Orla Come on, you two.

Orla, Andy and Siu Jing sit down.

DJ Cool Cheers to Erin! There's nothing like finally being legal.

Beattie Some of us surely don't look it, but some of us like it that way, eh, Andy?

Marianne Pass the vodka. (*Pours a shot – downs it. Pours another.*) Fuck it, let's get fucked.

DJ Cool Easy, Tiger.

Vershinin I'll have a vodka, too.

Simon Curry and vodka – tomorrow morning we'll all have the squits.

Erin You are disgusting.

Orla Has everyone got a bit of everything? There's more rice here, and naan bread. Anyone? And remember we've chocolate cake for dessert.

Siu Jing I don't know how you people eat like such pigs.

Beattie sings the opening lines of 'I'm Too Sexy'.
Laughter.

Andy Would everyone just stop it! Your joke's wearing very thin.

Laughter.

Seriously. I'm being serious.

Erin (*to Vershinin*) You're staying for the cake, aren't you?

Vershinin If I may.

Erin Yes, you have to.

Marianne sings the opening lines of The Velvet Underground, 'Pale Blue Eyes'.

DJ Cool Erin! Who's going to get a birthday kiss tonight, then?

Beattie Well, from where I'm sitting I can see someone who's going to be getting a whole lot more than just a birthday kiss.

Laughter.
Siu Jing gets up and runs from the table.
Andy runs after her.

Andy It's OK! Ignore them. Hang on – please – don't go –

Siu Jing I so ashamed. Why they laugh at me? Always, they laugh and laugh. It is rude to leave I know but I no stay – I no stay –

She hides her face with her hands.

Andy My love – please – they're only having a laugh, I promise. They're not laughing *at* you – there's a difference – And the thing is they're laughing at me, really, anyway – Come here, where they can't see us.

Siu Jing They still laughing. I no used to your kind of party. I so shy – so shy.

Andy Oh my poor poor sweet princess! Oh my poor love! Come here to me – My heart feels like it's going to burst. I never knew it was possible to feel this way – They can't see us, nobody can see us, I promise – My love – my poor sweet love – I love you – I love you so much – more than anyone's ever loved anyone – Ngor oi neih – ga bey ngor – is that right? – Ley yiu ga bey ngor ma?

Siu Jing (*laughing*) Ley yiu ga bey ngor ma? Ley D gwong dung wa ho char, ley hai mm hai seung kiu ngor ga bey ley ar? Yan wai ngor wah ley teng, ley jan hai mm wui seung gi ley tao seen hai doh gong D mut! (妳要嫁給我嗎? 你的廣東話好差, 你係唔係想叫我嫁比你呀? 因為我話你聽, 你真係唔會想知你頭先係度講的.) [I think that's the worst Cantonese accent I've ever heard. Are you trying to ask me to marry you? Because I don't think you want to know what you're actually saying!]

Andy You're going to have to answer me in English. That's all the Cantonese I've learned so far. But I'll do better. I promise. You make me want to be a better person. You make me want to be the best I can possibly be. You haven't answered my question yet.

Siu Jing You are sweet boy. You are so kind to me. You make me laugh. Hai, Andy. Hai (是). My answer is yes.

They kiss.

44

Teddy and Rod enter.

Rod Teddy and Rod is in da house! Sir. Sir.

Teddy Sorry we're late. Got held up – false alarm.

Rod Totally shit, man, I'm telling you.

Teddy But here we are now.

Rod Happy birthday, birthday girl.

Teddy And now it's time to get this party started!

Rod (*taking out a camera*) Hang on, everyone – say cheese!

All Cheese.

Rod And again – give us your best Gorgonzola!

Act Two

Two years later: 1995.

    July. Evening. Heavy rain. The sound of marching bands.

    Siu Jing enters. She is checking that all of the windows and the conservatory doors are closed and locked.

Siu Jing Andy-pandy? Where are you? Andy-pandy? What are you at?

    Andy stands up, book in hand.

Andy What is it, Siu Jing?

Siu Jing Reading, reading. Why you alway reading? You think you find the whole of life in books? This, my love – this is life – here, now!

Andy You reckon? (*Pause.*) What is it, anyway?

Siu Jing I checking the windows. Someone always leave them open. Last night at midnight I check and one window open, this much open. I tell them, every day I tell them, but someone no listen. What time is it?

Andy Just gone eight.

Siu Jing Gone eight and no Orla, no Erin. You think they safe? Whole country shut down – why they work? I tell Orla this morning – why you work? Whole country shut. You not worry?

Andy They'll be fine.

Siu Jing But what if they're not? (*Pause.*) Gone eight you say? I check on Bobby next. I worry about Bobby. He so cold. Yesterday temperature, today cold.

Andy There's nothing wrong with him, Siu Jing. He's fine.

Siu Jing Maybe he have allergy. Maybe I put him on diet. Too much milk in this country. Too much cheese. It no healthy. Smell like feet. How you eat something that smell like feet? Tomorrow he start. Andy? No soldier here tonight. I see on news – girls who have soldier boyfriend have hair chop off, strip naked, tie to lamp post, cover in – black and feather. And she the lucky one! Other, they have to leave country – they told they be shot – they family shot. You hear me?

Andy That sort of thing doesn't happen in this part of town.

Siu Jing This morning our prince open his eyes and smile at me. He *know* me. Jo san (好耐見), Bobby, I say. Ho loy mo geen! Sik jo faan mei ar (食飯未呀)? And he laugh – he understand. He understand everything. Please, Andy-pandy: no soldier. For Bobby. For your son.

Andy Well, that's up to my sisters, really –

Siu Jing So I tell them. Is different, now there is baby. They understand. (*Pause.*) You eat steam vegetable and rice tonight, Andy. No takeaway, OK? Otherwise you no lose weight. (*Stops. Looks outside.*) It so cold and rainy here all year, even summer. Bobby too cold. His room too cold. Erin room have sun all day. Maybe he go there, she go share with Orla. You think she mind? They never here, only to sleep . . . (*Pause. Softly.*) Andy?

Andy Yep.

Siu Jing Andy-pandy pudding-and-pie. Why you no speak?

Andy No reason. Just thinking. Anyway, there's nothing to say.

Siu Jing OK. OK, I go now check on Bobby.

Siu Jing leaves.
Andy stands.
The sound of a mother singing a wordless lullaby to a baby.
Andy leaves.
Marianne and Vershinin enter.

Marianne No one's ever asked me that before.

Pause.

I suppose you just – get used to things? And you stop trying to –
So we grew up on Army bases, or in Army accommodation – everyone around us was something to do with the Army. Army children, Army wives. We stopped making local friends because we knew that sooner or later we'd always have to move on. And when Mum died and Dad moved us all back here – we never fitted in. Even when we tried to dress the same, speak the same, as everyone else. Deep down, we were different. So you just sort of – lock it all away.

Vershinin My God I'm starving.

Marianne We'll get something when Orla gets back, takeaway or something . . . But let me just finish, I was going to say about my husband, I was so young when I met him, I mean I was still in school – and he was like this celebrity, me and my sisters used to listen to his programme every night. He used to take requests, play love songs, read out real-life stories . . . We thought he was the coolest thing ever. He used to wear sunglasses. How many people do you see wearing sunglasses in Belfast?

Vershinin Yes, I can imagine: not many.

Marianne I don't even know what I'm trying to say. I suppose what I mean is – it's so hard to be different here! As soon as someone meets you they're trying to get the measure of you, even if they don't realise they're doing it. What's your name? Where do you live? Where did you go to school? And if your name is 'Marianne', but your dad was in the British Army, and he was English, but Catholic – they don't know what to do with you. They don't quite trust you. After a while it just grinds you down and you stop having much to do with anyone.

Vershinin I hear what you're saying. We're living through one of the most extraordinary moments in history and all day every day, all I hear are complaints and accusations and threats. What was it Mother Teresa said? 'You haven't suffered enough.'

Marianne You're in a bad mood tonight.

Vershinin Ah. Maybe I am. I haven't eaten a thing since breakfast. My daughter's been acting up, and when my daughters act up I get incredibly stressed and start blaming myself for giving them a mother like that. You should have seen her this morning! Oh, she's pathetic. We were yelling at each other from the moment we woke up and it went on and on until I slammed the door and left.

Pause.

I couldn't say any of this to anyone else, you know.

He kisses her.

I'm sorry. Don't be mad at me. You're all I have. Truly. You're all that matters to me.

Pause.

Marianne Oh God, there's a magpie at the window. It's gone now. Good day Mister Magpie, how's your wife and children!

Vershinin What?

Marianne It's what you're supposed to say, if you see a magpie. To ward off the bad luck.

Vershinin You believe that?

Marianne I don't know. Why take the risk? There was a magpie at that window on the day Dad died.

Vershinin I had no idea you were superstitious. You are adorable.

He kisses her.

I have heard tell of another Irish superstition, you know. I heard . . . that fairies walk among us, in disguise, disguised, in fact, as beautiful women with long dark hair and big green eyes . . .

He is kissing her.

Marianne Silly . . . Don't stop . . .

Vershinin I love, love, love your eyes. I love the way you look at me – the way you move – I dream about you, you know. The things you do to me . . .

Marianne Sorry, I'm not laughing – I just – I can't breathe, my breath is stuck, right here – and my heart – can you feel –
Oh God, someone's coming.

Erin and Baron enter.

Baron I wish you wouldn't call me 'Baron', you know. OK, OK, so that's what everyone else calls me but I've always hated it, such a stupid nickname. I wish you would call me by my real name, even if you're the only one who ever does.

Erin I am wrecked.

Baron I'm going to collect you from the airport every single day of the summer. It's as if you're really coming back from somewhere – and there I am, to meet you and bring you home.

He sees Vershinin and Marianne.

Oh hello!

Erin Finally home. (*To Marianne.*) I thought that shift would never end. There was a woman today turned up for a flight to London – her son had just died over there. But the flight was closing – there's no way she'd've got through security and to the gate in time. I had to tell her, No. And she cried and cried and begged me – and in the end I was so rude to her. 'What d'you want me to do?' I said to her. 'Nothing's going to change anything, is it?' (*Sits down.*) I am so wrecked.

Baron When you get home from work you're so little – I just want to pick you up and put you in my pocket.

Pause.

Erin God I'm wrecked. I can't stand the airport.

Marianne You've lost weight since you started there. Makes you look younger. Like a wee urchin.

Baron It's her hair, too.

Erin I'm going to look for a different job. I thought it would be so romantic, working at an airport, all the flights, seeing the Departures board with all the destinations – but it's just stuck in front of a stupid computer all day and people being rude to you.

A knock on the conservatory doors.

There's Uncle Beattie, he stops by every bloody night now. (*To Baron.*) Let him in, will you, I can't be bothered . . .

Baron goes to open the conservatory door.

We have to do something you know. He and Andy were at it again last night, apparently. Apparently Andy lost five hundred quid.

Marianne I don't know what we're supposed to do about it.

Beattie comes in.

Beattie Hello-hello, hello-hello.

He sits down and takes the newspaper out of his jacket, starts studying the horses.

Erin Last week he lost loads too, and the week before that. If only he'd go crazy and lose everything, we wouldn't have a choice, we'd have to go. God, I dream about America every night! It's driving me mad! This time next year, we'll be there. It's just so long to wait . . .

Marianne Just make sure Jenny doesn't find out about Andy.

Erin I honestly don't think she gives a shit about him. The only person she cares about is Prince Bobby.

Marianne Talking of money – did he ever pay you back?

Erin Not a penny.

Marianne Look at him sitting there on his throne.

They laugh.
Pause.

Erin What's up, Alex?

Vershinin Oh, nothing, just one of those days. I haven't had a thing to eat since this morning.

Beattie (*laying down his newspaper*) Erin!

Erin What is it?

Beattie Come here, wee pet.

Erin goes over.

You're all I have in the world, have I ever told you that?

Erin starts dealing cards for his game of patience.

Vershinin Talk, someone! Take my mind off things.

Baron Yessir! What shall we talk about?

Vershinin About life! About life here in two, three hundred years, long after we're all gone.

Baron OK. Well. We'll teleport everywhere – and we'll wear these special, like space suits – if they haven't invented invisibility cloaks by then. We'll be able to communicate just by thought – you won't need telephones or letters or anything, you'll just think the thought and zap, it'll be in the other person's head. (*Pause.*) And despite all of that, life will be exactly the same. Nothing anyone can invent can make us any happier. Even if you can zap your own thoughts in, you still won't know what's going on in someone else's head. Even if you can teleport right to someone's side any time you want – they still might not want you there. And even if you lived for a thousand years, you'd still have to die eventually.

Vershinin (*thinks*) OK. How can I put this. I believe that every day, every moment, things are changing for the better. Even when it doesn't always seem that way to us. In two, three hundred years – in a thousand years – there'll be a whole new world, and life will be happy. We won't be there to see it, of course – but we are living for it now, living and dying for it, suffering for it, imagining it bit by bit into being. Happiness. That's the point of all of our suffering.

Marianne laughs quietly.

Baron Why are you laughing?

Marianne I don't know. I've been laughing all day.

Vershinin (*to Baron*) I didn't have the education you had. I didn't learn Latin, or Greek. I didn't even go to university. The things I've learned, I've taught myself, from books. There are so many books that I'll never read, so much that I'll never know. The older I get – and I'm getting old now, properly old – the more I realise how little I know. But the one thing I do know is that there's no such thing as happiness, not for us, not here, not now. It's an illusion – something to keep us striving. Happiness belongs to the future – to the generations yet unborn.

Pause.

'The generations yet unborn.'

Baron OK, but what if – sitting here, right now – I'm happy?

Vershinin Ah, but you're not.

54

Baron (*laughs*) What can I say? The basis of your entire argument is flawed. 'I'm not happy, therefore happiness does not exist.'

Marianne laughs quietly.

Listen. Two, three hundred years from now – a thousand – a million – it doesn't matter. Life is essentially the same. Governed by the same immutable laws and forces, which we'll never fully understand. Think of the starlings over the Albert Bridge every evening – wheeling round and round in huge great masses – they don't know why they do it, they probably don't even think about what they're doing, they just do it. They swoop and dip and swoop and dip . . .

Marianne But there's a point to it.

Baron A point? Look, it's pissing it down – again. What's the point in that?

Pause.

Marianne I think that we have to believe in something, or at least try to believe – otherwise life is pointless. What's the point of the starlings in the evening – the stars in the sky – of babies being born – if none of it matters? If everything is pointless, why bother with anything, why bother living?

Pause.

Vershinin All the same, I wish I was young again.

Marianne 'Life's a bitch and then you die.'

Beattie And then the worms eat you: be thankful it happens in that order.

Pause.
Erin sings the first few lines from Ash, 'Girl From Mars'.

Baron Well, I've been waiting for the moment to tell you all, and now's as good a time as any. I've resigned my commission. Requested an honourable discharge.

Marianne Erin said. Are you sure it's the right decision? I mean, what will you do now?

Baron Whatever . . . I'll find something, I'm sure . . . Look, I've done three tours now. I don't want life to pass me by. I want to see the world, and not just through a fucking Saracen, or through a lens . . . (*Mimes a rifle.*) You can't just wait, you have to – (*Standing up.*) Carpe diem!

Erin Alright, O Captain my Captain, take it easy.

The doorbell rings.

Baron I'll get it. I need a breath of air.

Baron leaves.

Erin Look, the cards are working out. That means we will be going to America.

Beattie You've put the eight on the ten of spades there. You're not going anywhere yet. Besides, what would I do without you, wee pet! You wouldn't pass us a wee biscuit, would you?

Erin There are none. Psycho Simon ate them all.

Beattie All of them?

Erin Yup. Weirdo.

Marianne I wish this rain would stop. D'you know if we lived in America I don't think I'd even care about the rain. When we get to America I'm going to tap-dance my way down the street every single time it rains.

Vershinin I've been reading Nelson Mandela's book – *Long Walk to Freedom*. He writes so joyfully about a little bird that used to come to perch on the edge of his cell window – a bird he'd never have noticed before Robben Island. Now that he's free, he barely notices the birds any more. It'll be the same with you. 'The American dream'.

Baron comes back in.

Baron Sir . . . It's your wife. She's in hospital. There's a car waiting.

Vershinin goes to him. Baron says a few words.

Vershinin Oh, not again. The same old story! Always the same old story.

Marianne What is it? Is everything OK?

Pause.

Vershinin I have to go.

He goes to her.
He leaves.

Beattie He quare got his skates on didn't he!

Marianne Shut up. Can you ever just shut up! You hang around here every fucking night saying stupid fucking things – I'm sick of you. I'm sick to death of all of you. I'm sick of these bloody card games.

She swipes the cards off the table.

Erin What did you go and do that for?

Marianne Shut up, just shut the fuck up, don't talk to me, don't touch me, just leave me alone.

Beattie I'd take her advice if I were you.

Siu Jing enters.

Siu Jing Mui mui (妹妹), please, I just finally get Bobby back to sleep.

Marianne I don't fucking care about –

Siu Jing Please!

Baron Come on, folks. Come on.

Marianne Fuck this. Fuck all of it.

She goes to leave. She doesn't leave. She goes to the French windows.

Siu Jing What is the problem, is something wrong?

No one says anything.

All this shouting like fishwife. Why you always shout like fishwife? Is no attractive, you know.

A baby's cry from the monitor that Siu Jing is holding.

There. You wake Bobby. He no well, you know. Please try to –

Siu Jing leaves.
Silence.

Marianne (*quietly*) Fuck all of this.

Baron Well, I don't know about you, but – I need a fag.

He leaves through the conservatory.

Erin Marianne –

Erin goes to Marianne.
Baron sits down by Simon, who has been lurking by the door.

Baron You're always hanging about here. Come on, mate, what's the story?

Simon Why does there always have to be a story? We're not characters in a film.

Baron Well if we were, it wouldn't be a rom-com, I'll tell you that much.

He lights a cigarette, offers one to Simon.

Simon No way. Know what that's doing to you? Eleven minutes. Every cigarette you smoke. Your life's eleven minutes shorter than before you lit that.

Baron Ah well, life's too long anyway.

Simon Is that what you think? Ha – what do they call that? An omen, that's what that is.

Baron Take it easy, mate.

Pause.

Simon I'm not your mate, I know I'm not. I know you laugh at me. I know you all laugh at me. But I'm better than you. And I'm going to prove it.

Baron I take the piss out of you sometimes, I admit it. But you ask for it. Look, mate – pax. OK? Pax. Let's get drunk.

He takes out a hip flask. He drinks. Simon drinks.

Simon Live fast, die young.

Simon sprays himself with Cool Water.

Baron (*drinks*) I'm resigning my commission, you know. Ya basta! I'm through.

Simon Why?

Baron Why? They're going to pull us all out of here soon anyway. They sent another four hundred home today. I've had it with the Army. Being sent places. No say over where you go, how long you stay for.

Simon Join the Army – see the world – meet interesting people – kill them.

Baron For once, mate, you're not far wrong.

Inside, Andy appears and sits down in a corner.
Baron finishes his cigarette.

Come on. You're getting soaked out here.

He and Simon go inside.
Baron is drunk.

Right folks. Who needs a drink?

Siu Jing enters again.

Siu Jing He's asleep again. I tell him – Bobby, they sorry about noise, they go to be quiet now – and he look at me with his big eyes and with his eyes say, 'Thank you, Mummy.' He understand. I know every parent think their baby special –

Marianne (*rolling her eyes*) But Bobby really is.

Baron He's a wee dote, Jenny.

Simon What's pink and red and a bit of a blur?

Siu Jing What you say?

Baron Mate –

Simon A baby in a blender. What's red, bubbling, and scratches at the window? A baby in a microwave. How do you get a baby out of a blender? With tortilla chips.

Siu Jing You sick in the head. I want you out of here. Get out! Go! (*To Andy.*) I said no soldiers!

Simon pretends to run from the room.

Erin You psycho.

Simon Psycho, yeah? Well – if that's what you call me, that's what you're gonna get.

Erin You always have to take things too far, don't you?

Baron picks up the guitar. He starts strumming Oasis, 'Wonderwall'.
Siu Jing is close to tears.

Siu Jing Enough. Please. I have had enough. Out! (*To Andy.*) Get them out!

Siu Jing leaves.
Baron sings. He is very drunk.
Andy gets up.

Andy Alright, folks.

Andy goes to Baron and stops him from playing.

Party's over . . .

Baron Party's over? What do you mean, man, I was just getting started!

Andy Bobby's not himself, or so she says, and so, well, you know . . .

Erin (*rolling her eyes*) 'Bobby's not himself.'

Marianne Right, well! We've had our marching orders! I've had it with this place, anyway. I want to get wasted. Come on.

Marianne links arms with Baron.

Baron (*to Simon*) Come on, man.

Marianne and Baron and Simon leave.
Beattie is taking his time getting up, getting his coat on.

Andy Hurry up.

Beattie The night is young.

Andy If my wife comes back, she might stop me going out. You're lucky you never married. Being married is shit.

Beattie So is being alone.

Andy Whatever. I'm not going to play tonight, just watch. I have this horrible tight feeling in my chest. Do you ever get that?

Beattie Haven't a clue, son.

Andy OK, come on then.

Andy and Beattie leave.
Erin is alone. She stands.
Simon enters.

Simon There you are! Come on.

Erin I'm not coming.

Simon Why not?

Erin I don't want to.

Pause.

Goodbye, Simon.

Simon I was a bit of a cunt earlier, that thing I said about the baby. I didn't mean it. You know that, don't you? You're not like the rest of them. You're better than them. You're the only one who understands me. Forgive me.

Erin OK! Fine, I 'forgive' you, whatever. Now seriously –

Simon Thank you. You know what this means to me, right? I couldn't leave here – there's no way I could leave here – knowing that you were mad at me.

Erin I'm not mad at you. Now please –

Simon Don't ask me to go. Erin, I – I can't live without you. You and me – we're meant to be. I know it! I've known it since the first time I saw you. I love you, Erin. I love, love, love –

Erin Stop it.

Simon No. I won't. I can't.

Erin Seriously. Stop it. You're creeping me out.

Simon I'm –
But that's not how it goes. You're not meant to say that. You're meant to say – (*He rubs his head.*) Whatever. I can't force you to love me. But I can make sure no one else ever does.

Siu Jing enters.

Siu Jing Why you still here? Go, go!

Simon Whatever. I'll be back.

He goes.

Siu Jing You OK?

Erin I'm fine.

Siu Jing Why you friends with him?

Erin I'm not.

Siu Jing Well he gone now. They all gone – finally. Bobby no well, Erin. Tossing, turning. I mean to say. Bobby room so cold, so damp. Your room so nice for baby. You mind if – I move Bobby cot to your room?

Erin What?

Siu Jing Just for a few night, to see if it make difference. You sleep in Orla room for time being. Is OK?

Erin Fine, whatever.

Siu Jing Thank you. Mui mui. (妹妹). One day you have baby of your own and you understand! He so sweet, Bobby. I say to him: 'You mine, Bobby! You all mine!' And he look at me with his big eyes. He so clever that baby. He understand – everything!

Erin Yeah.

Siu Jing turns the lights out and leaves.
Erin stands.
Orla enters.

Orla Oh my God my head is killing me, it's like I have this hot metal band – pulled tight – just here. If I have to hear Vivaldi's Spring one more time I think I'm going to scream. I'm going to bed. Thank God we're finally off for a few days, I never thought I'd be so grateful for the Twelfth of July, I'm going to stay in bed all day long. Don't let anyone wake me. Oh my God, my head . . .

She leaves.

Erin Orla . . .

Erin stands.
The sound of a lullaby.
A tap on the conservatory door. It is Vershinin and DJ Cool.

DJ Cool We didn't want to ring the door and wake the baby. Why is it so dark in here? Where is everyone?

Erin They've all gone out.

Vershinin I've barely been gone any time at all

DJ Cool What, Marianne's gone out? Without me? But she said –

Erin I don't care what she said, I'm so wrecked, just give me a break.

Pause.

DJ Cool I just don't understand – I said we'd go home together, after my show. She must have gone on home, mustn't she?

Erin Yeah.

DJ Cool In which case – I'm going to make like a shepherd and get the flock out of here.

Vershinin Come for a drink with me. They're keeping my wife in overnight, as a precaution, the girls are at my neighbours – I can't go back to my house alone. Ah, come on.

DJ Cool Another time, buddy. See ya later, alligator.

He leaves.

Vershinin So it's just me, myself, and I. What a night.

Vershinin leaves.
Erin stands.

Erin 'Beam me up, Scotty!' (*Pause.*) They don't even bloody say that, do they, according to Andy. Oh God, I need to get out of here!

Act Three

Three years later: 1998.

July, night time. The sound of rioting, then helicopters overhead.

Orla and Erin.

Erin But why here?

I mean of all the possible places, why would he bring them here?

Orla It's a big house, we've room, we're the logical place.

Erin But –

Orla Come on. You know why here.

Erin I know, but –

Orla Well then. Come on. We've got lots to do.

Pause.

Erin I just don't know what he thinks he's doing.

Marianne enters.

Marianne Is he still here?

Orla No. He had to go back, to –

Marianne Is he coming back soon?

Pause.

Erin He didn't say.

Marianne And they're – here?

Orla They're upstairs.

Siu Jing enters.

Siu Jing They're saying on the radio it's the worst night of rioting since the ceasefires. They say the peace process may be destabilised. Vehicles hijacked, buildings smashed, houses petrol-bombed, police officers injured, millions of pounds of damage – why? I am asking a serious question: why?

Orla I wish I could tell you, Jenny. I wish to God I could tell you.
Right, girls. Come on.
(*Taking clothes from the wardrobe.*) Give Mrs Vershinin this, and this. She's got to put something on or she'll catch her death. And those wee girls, wrap them up in this, they'll be cold from the shock. Do you know how much damage there was to their house?

The helicopters very close overhead.

I am sick of this! Sick of this bloody country.

She gives Erin the clothes.

Well here you go, go on.

Erin leaves.
Silence.

Siu Jing One of those girls has a cough, she mustn't go near Sophie. There is a nasty flu going round. At least Bobby and Sophie are fast asleep. They've slept right through it all, poor innocent things. Orla, I dread the day I have to tell them. The day they ask questions, and I have no answers.

Silence.

(*At Marianne.*) Look at her, lying there with two arms the same length. We're all tired, Marianne! I have two babies and a house to run. Do you see me lying down! Help your sister, for once. Go on! Get up!

Marianne gets up and goes out.

Orla You have to understand, Jenny –

Siu Jing What?

Orla Mimi's having a hard time at the minute.

Siu Jing Hard time! (*On the verge of tears.*) I have two babies and a house full of people. I get up when Bobby wakes at six and I don't go to bed until midnight and I'm up all through the night with Sophie. That is a hard time!

Orla OK, whatever. I don't have the energy for this. I think I've aged a decade tonight.

Siu Jing I'm so tired, Orla. Every day, I wake up more tired than the day before. Every day, this country, it –
  Look. I don't want bad energy around the children. They so innocent – they so sweet – no bad energy. Marianne allowed to stay in that mood – she bring us all down. Do you understand?

Orla Yes, Jenny.

Siu Jing Good. I don't want us to fight. There is too much fighting outside the house.

Pause. Siu Jing wipes her eyes and adjusts her hair in the mirror.

They say you never get your figure back after a second baby.

Orla You look – fine.

Siu Jing leaves.
  DJ Cool enters.

DJ Cool Knock-knock. Where's Marianne? I don't know why she was so hell bent on heading over here. We should head home. The worst of it seems under control now, thank God. For a while there it was looking like the whole city would go up in flames. Back to the bad old days.

Siu Jing leaves.
  DJ Cool enters.

Ah, Orla.
  Have I ever told you there should be a song named 'Orla'?

Orla You have not.

DJ Cool To the tune of 'Mandy'. Ah, you can't argue with Barry Manilow now.

Orla You're a right eejit, you are.

Beattie comes blundering in.

DJ Cool Did someone call for the cavalry?

Orla It'll be Uncle Beattie. He's completely stocious. Two years on the wagon, and tonight of all nights he decides to start drinking again. Give me strength.

She leaves.

DJ Cool We should hide, and then jump out at him. Wouldn't that be a laugh! That'd shock him sober!

DJ Cool leaves.
  Beattie enters. She goes over to the sink and drinks from the tap.

Beattie Fuck 'em! Fuck 'em all. That's what I say.
  Thirty years, I've worked as a hospital porter. Thought I'd seen it all. Last night – they called me to take a wee

girl to surgery. Beautiful, she was. Couldn't have been more than thirty. Dark hair, pale skin, big green eyes. We had a good auld chat on the way. 'What are you in for,' says I, and says she, 'What am I not in for – I'm rotten to the core. A bad apple, that's me.' 'Ah, come on now,' says I. 'A beautiful thing like you.' 'Beautiful,' she says, 'that's a good one. My own fiancé can hardly bring himself to look at me any more.' 'Well then, more fool him,' says I. 'Tell me a joke,' she says, and I tell her about my first day when I was sent to the operating theatre to collect a pair of Fallopian tubes. Tell me another. Alrighty. A patient leps up from the gurney and sprints away just as he's being taken in for a big op. 'What's wrong?' they ask him. And here's him: 'The nurse said not to worry, it's only a simple operation, it'll all be fine.' 'And what's wrong with that?' 'She was talking to the surgeon!' So we have a bit of a chuckle and then out of nowhere she asks me to hold her hand. Afterwards I told the other fellas and we had a right old laugh. You're well in there, boy, they said. Next thing the call comes to take her to the morgue. I moved the sheet to get a look at her. They hadn't sewn her up again, on account of they'd have to do the autopsy. There she was, blood and guts. A slab of meat on a trolley. Wormfood. Oh, I felt sick as a dog then. Her white face grinning up at me like the biggest joke of all was on me. I don't know why – for it was nothing I hadn't seen before – but Christ, it put the heart crossways in me. I shouldn't have told the fellas about the hand-holding, it was something better than a cheap geg, something you shoulda kept private. I knew that at the time, I don't even know why I did it. I decided then and there I needed a drink. Saw out the shift then straight to the offy.

He slumps to the floor.
Erin, Vershinin and Baron enter.

Erin Your wife and girls are asleep so we'll sit in here for a bit. Oh! Peace at last.

Vershinin To peace. 'Peace cannot be kept by force; it can only be achieved by understanding.' That's Albert Einstein. And yet. Where would we be tonight if it wasn't for the law enforcement?

DJ Cool enters.

DJ Cool Gee-whizzle, folks, it's Piccadilly Circus in here tonight. Anyone have the time?

Baron It's gone three. It'll be getting light soon.

Erin What on earth are you at? And what's he doing in here? You should go to bed, Uncle Beattie.

Beattie I'm perfectly fine, thanking you kindly.

He stands up and dusts himself down. Picks up a clock with elaborate care.

DJ Cool He's pissed as a fart. He's poleaxed! He's steaming. However many words we have to describe extreme drunkenness, and I bet we have more than the Eskimos have words for snow, he's all of them. Fair play to you, mate. Any of you seen Marianne?

Baron I heard her singing. She's got a beautiful voice.

DJ Cool A woman of many talents, my wife. I'm a lucky, lucky man.

Pause.

Vershinin I am utterly filthy. I'm glad I can't see myself right now.

Pause.

Well – it's ironic that in my final weeks here I should be bombed out of my own house. I wonder where life

71

will take me next. Yugoslavia, most likely. The former Yugoslavia. The Middle East. Bring it on. (*To Baron.*) Your old regiment is leaving soon.

Baron So I hear.

Erin And we're leaving, too.

Vershinin Times they are a-changing.

Beattie holds the clock aloft then drops it.

Beattie Smash! And with that, time's at a standstill.

DJ Cool Whoa, man. Take a chill pill. What did you do that for?

Erin That was Mum's clock.

Beattie Ah, but what use is it to her now? 'Time, gentlemen!' 'Drink your fill and drown your sorrows, we'll all be dead this time tomorrow!'

He leaves.
Pause.

Vershinin What a night. When the petrol bomb came through the window I ran upstairs and grabbed my girls, one in each arm, and even in that short space of time the living room had gone up in flames and the hallway was full of smoke, so I had to bundle them out of the kitchen window. Their little faces, white with terror – it damn near broke my heart. And my wife didn't help matters, she was screaming like a banshee, and the sirens, and policemen in full riot gear yelling, and my little girls just clutching at me, utterly panic-stricken – My God, I thought, what else does life have in store for them? And I couldn't think where to bring them and so I brought them here.

Marianne enters and sits down.

And do you know, seeing them there – barefoot in the street, in their little nightdresses, while our house burned behind them, the air thick with smoke, the sirens, the screaming – it suddenly occurred to me they could have been my parents, or their parents, in the pogroms of the thirties, or 1919 . . . We think we're civilised, we think we've come so far. But people in two, three hundred years are going to look back on the twentieth century, on the First World War and the Second, on the Cold War, on Vietnam, on the Gulf War and the Bosnian War and the Troubles and Rwanda and the countless other conflicts and they're going to think – how barbaric we were. How utterly barbaric. Things will be so different then. Life will be – (*He laughs.*) Oh, listen to me. 'Get a grip,' that's what you're thinking. 'Catch yourself on'. I'm sorry. I can't help it.

Pause.

Have they all nodded off? Then they won't mind if I go on. Ah, if only we could have a glimpse of what the future holds! We might be the only ones like us in the country – in the entire world. But even if we think our life and love is in vain it can never be in vain. After us will come more, and more, who live and love and think as we do, and a time will come when life on earth will be beautiful, and it will have started here, with us, when we first imagined it into being . . . Oh, I'm in a strange, wild mood tonight. I want to live as if I really was going to die tomorrow.

He sings the first few lines of Leonard Cohen, 'I'm Your Man'. Marianne joins in.
    Simon appears in the doorway. He sings and dances to the chorus of Cyndi Lauper, 'Disco Inferno'.

Erin (*startling awake*) What the fuck? No – you're not coming in here. No. I mean it. Fuck off.

Simon How come he's allowed in here and I'm not?

Vershinin We should all go, leave Erin in peace. How are things?

Simon Under control. (*Mimes using a water cannon.*) Stopped by to tell you. (*Sprays himself with Cool Water.*) He's allowed and I'm not – that's fucked up.

Vershinin 'If you want a lover . . .'

Marianne 'I'll do anything you ask me to . . .'

Vershinin (*to Simon*) Come on.

Simon OK – but I'm not going to forget this. Fucking Gordonstoun fucking ponce.

Vershinin and Simon leave.

Erin That weirdo has stunk the room out. The Baron slept through the entire thing. Baron!

Baron wakes up.

Baron I was on a stage – in front of thousands of people – TV cameras – lights – and they were all waiting for me to begin – but it was my life they were watching and I didn't know the words. (*To Erin.*) You are so, so beautiful. You look so pale and thin tonight. So sad – so, so sad. Like a changeling. You don't belong here. Nor do I. Let's run away together. I mean it. Let's start again . . .

Marianne Baron . . . it's almost morning. You'd best be on your way.

Baron (*laughing*) Oh God, you're here too, I didn't realise . . . OK, goodnight – or should I say good morning – I'm going, I'm going.

He kisses Erin's cheek.

Oh Erin, I look at you now and it all comes back to me, your eighteenth birthday, and we were talking about how we were going to be someone, and we were going to make a difference . . . How has it been five years? That's – half a decade. Oh no, you're crying, I didn't mean to make you cry, I'm sorry . . . Go to sleep, get some rest. I would die for you.

Marianne Baron . . .

Baron I'm already gone.

He leaves.

Marianne Dave . . . are you sleeping?

DJ Cool Huh?

Marianne We should go.

DJ Cool Marianne . . . Love of my life . . .

He sings the first few lines of Queen, 'Love of My Life'.

Erin Oh give it a rest.

Marianne Life isn't a cheesy fucking love song 24–7.

DJ Cool She cracks me up. We got married seven years ago but I swear it feels like yesterday. I have never been happier.

Marianne Well I am so fucking bored. Seven years? I'd've said seventy.

She sits up.

And being back here, I can't stop thinking – like someone's drilling it into my brain – how unfair it all is. I mean about Andy. He's re-mortgaged the house in his wife's name – but it's not even his house! It's all of our house – the four of us. He's a big fat turd, our brother.

75

DJ Cool There's no point getting yourself riled up about it, babe. You're not going to change anything.

Marianne Even so, it's a fucking disgrace, the way he's shafted us.

She lies back down.

DJ Cool We're fine, you and me. Local radio isn't prime-time telly, but it pays enough for me to take care of you and that's all that matters.

Marianne You just don't get it, do you?

Pause.

Go you on home.

DJ Cool You're all riled up. Why don't you get forty winks and then we'll go together. I'll wait outside. It's true you know. I have never been happier.

He kisses Marianne and leaves.

Erin What you were saying, about Andy? Remember when he was the star of his year and everyone was saying he'd be a professor by thirty. And now he's so fat and useless and he just sits in his room all day playing video games. It's such a waste. All of it! And I'm not just talking about him. (*Starting to cry.*) I can't take it any more. I can't. I can't go on like this.

Orla enters.

Someone put me out of my misery. I mean it! I can't take any more.

Orla What's wrong, wee hun? What's wrong?

Erin (*sobbing*) All of it – where has it all gone? Where? What's happened to us? Oh God, oh God – I've forgotten everything – and I used to mean it – I did – and now everything's got muddled up and I've let myself forget – I don't even remember what it feels like – and we're never going to get any of it back again, that's it, we've thrown it all away – And we're never going to go to America, I know we won't –

Orla Sweetheart, sweetheart . . .

Erin (*controlling herself*) I am so unhappy. I hated the airport, and so I got a job as a waitress, and I hated that, so I got the job at the dole office – and I hate that more than anything – all day surrounded by people who are desperate for something, anything – or worse they don't even care – and somehow years have gone by and I've lost my chance, I know it – I'm already too old, I can feel myself getting – shrivelled and cynical. Nothing makes me happy – nothing – I haven't found anything that's worth living for. It's like – I'm sinking into some bottomless pit, and I can't claw myself back out – and part of me doesn't even want to – and I should just kill myself and put an end to it all, I don't know why I haven't already . . .

Orla Don't cry, wee love, don't cry. I can't bear seeing you like this.

Erin I'm not crying. I'm not. Come on. There. No more tears. See?

Orla Erin . . . Come here to me. Listen. Not just as your sister – as a friend. As someone who's been there. You should say yes to the Baron.

Erin weeps.

Seriously – I know he's no Brad Pitt but he's kind. That's way more important. He'd do anything for you. And you like him, you trust him, he makes you laugh – He'll look after you. He'll go wherever you want to go.

I would. If someone asked me – if I had the chance –
I would. Seriously.

Erin It's been in my head for years, we'll get to America
and I'll meet my soul mate there – Sometimes I actually
see him in my dreams, and I wake up and it's like – he's
so close – that sounds so fucking stupid, doesn't it –

Orla (*hugs her*) Oh sweetheart, oh my poor wee love,
I know exactly what you mean. See when the Baron first
left the Army, and he turned up here in that suit and
hideous tie, on the way to some crappy job interview?
I could have cried for him. I had to stop myself from
yelling at him: 'What have you done! You're throwing it
all away!' Because he did it for you. You do know that,
don't you? He did it all for you.

Silence.
Siu Jing enters, checking and locking every single
one of the doors and windows.
She exits.

Marianne What do you call a fat Chinese person? A
Chunk.

Orla For fuck's sake, Marianne.

Erin Don't shout, Lala, she was only joking.

Orla She should know better. She should think for half
a minute about how hard it is to be any sort of different
around here. And I'm not just talking about – oh, 'I have
an English father and a Protestant mother' different. I'm
talking about bring *different*. I'm talking about –

Silence.

Marianne There's something I'm going to tell you, OK,
and I'm going to say it once and we'll never mention it

again. OK? I have to tell someone. It's killing me. Oh God. OK.

Pause.

I am completely and utterly in love with him. With Alex Vershinin. Alexander Vershinin is the love of my life.

Orla I'm not going to say anything, OK, I'm not saying anything.

Marianne I don't know what to do. At first I thought he was a bit of an eejit – then I felt sorry for him – and next thing I know, I'm falling in love. I'm in love with his voice – his words – in love with how sad he is – his two wee girls . . .

Orla I'm not saying anything.

Marianne He's my soul mate, Lala. He is. And I'm his. It just – is. I don't understand any of it, I just know we're meant to be together. How can that be wrong? I know, from the outside, it's such a cliché – but this is different, I swear, I don't even know how to put it – it's real – it's love. I just know it's meant to be. And I don't know what to do, except to trust in that. OK, now I've said it. That's it. Finito.

Andy's voice, off.

Andy I am sick of this! I am so fucking sick of this! Orla! (*He enters.*) Where's Orla? There you are. I need the key to the safe. I've lost mine. I know you have one.

Orla silently hands him the key.

What a night, eh?

Pause.

Why aren't you talking to me?

Pause.

I've had enough of this. Sulking about the place. Giving me the silent treatment. Go on: hit me with it. You too, Marianne – and you, Erin – what have I done to deserve it? I'm asking you. What?

Orla Just leave it, Andy. We'll discuss it tomorrow. Oh God, what a night!

Andy No. I'm asking you politely: what have I done? Go on. Tell me.

Vershinin, outside the window.

Vershinin 'If you want a lover . . .'

Marianne 'I'll do anything you ask me to!' I'm away. Bye, Lala. Don't let the bedbugs bite, you. And on you go, Andy, they're wiped out. We'll talk about it all tomorrow.

She leaves.

Orla Seriously, Andy, please. We'll do this tomorrow. Bedtime.

Andy Fine. But there's just one thing I want to say first. OK. You've got something against Siu Jing, my wife, and have done since the day I first brought her home. You pretend you can't say her name. You make constant, snide little jokes about her and at her expense. You call it banter but it's not banter. It's ugly and it's offensive and I've had enough. She's a good, kind, decent person. She's a good mother, and a good wife. OK? I love her and I respect her and it's about time you showed her some respect, too.

Pause.

OK. Next thing. You're pissed off with me because I'm not a professor. But I have a job in the Civil Service and

80

I am doing my bit for society, which is far more important than sitting in some ivory tower. It's in the name: civil *servant*. So if you must know, I am actually proud of myself.

Pause.

And thirdly. While we're on the subject, I have something else to say. I re-mortgaged the house without telling you. Yes, I should have told you, or rather I shouldn't have done it in the first place, but I had to. It was the only way to pay off my debts. I've stopped gambling now, I stopped ages ago. But in my defence: none of you have any idea of the pressure I was under.

Pause.
DJ Cool is in the doorway.

DJ Cool Marianne not here? That's weird – where's she gone?

He leaves.

Andy Is anyone listening to me? Siu Jing is a good, kind, decent person. (*Pause.*) I truly believed she was the love of my life. It was like a fairy tale. *(He weeps.)* Don't listen to me. Don't listen to a word I say. It's all bullshit, all of it.

He leaves.
DJ Cool is in the doorway again.

DJ Cool Seriously, folks, getting a wee bit worried here: I can't find Marianne anywhere?

He leaves.
Silence.
A sudden knocking.

Erin What was that?

Orla That'll be Uncle Beattie. Still stocious.

Erin What a night!

Pause.

Lala – did you hear – the Baron's old regiment is being withdrawn. That could have been him. Going to . . . wherever in the world they'll send them next. I wonder if he'll miss it. I wonder if he'll –

Pause.

Orla?

Orla What?

Erin I think you're right – what you said. He is kind, isn't he – and he always says he'd do anything for me. If I say yes to him – and ask him to go to America, you could come too, we could all go. Oh please, Lala! Please! Let's all go to America! Let's go!

Act Four

Shortly afterwards. The garden. A sunny afternoon.
  Lots of empty bottles of cava, beer, vodka.
  Baron, Teddy, Rod, Erin.
  Beattie is sitting reading a paper.

Rod Well, mate. We're gonna love ya and leave ya.

Teddy C'mere, Baron.

Teddy gives Baron a hug, slaps his back.

Baron I'm going to miss you. Both of you.

Rod (*wrestling Baron*) You've gone soft, Baron. We should call you Baroness.

Teddy Hope he ain't soft where it counts, know what I'm saying?

Rod Woo-hoo! Bet he is and all. Joke for ya, Baron. Newly married bloke, wedding night, bedroom. Says to the missus, 'Put my trousers on.' She does just that. He says, 'That'll be the last time in this relationship you wear the trousers.' Bloke's wife says, 'Alright. Put my panties on.' Bloke says, 'I can't get into them.' Bloke's wife says, 'And that's the way it'll stay, as long as you've got that attitude!'

Teddy 'I can't get into them' – That's a good one that is.

Rod Golden piece of advice, that is. Consider it – my parting gift. You're welcome, mate.

Teddy and Rod hug Baron again and slap him on the back.

Baron I'm glad you're not here for the wedding.

Rod Stay a moment longer in this shit-hole? No chance. (*To Erin.*) No offence.

Teddy Twenty-one hundred hours. Counting the minutes, I am.

Baron You'll have to come back and visit.

Rod You having a laugh?

Teddy No fucking way, mate. No fucking way.

Baron Keep in touch, though.

Rod Yeah, never happens though, does it. This is goodbye, mate.

Baron 'Goodbye'.

Teddy Watch it mate, you're gonna make him cry.

Rod Like the big ole pussy he is. (*To Erin.*) Sorry. Right, then. Let's be having ya.

Rod, Teddy, Baron embrace and backslap again.

Baron Goodbye. I'll miss you bastards.

Teddy We'll miss you, Baron – like a hole in the head!

Rod Alright then. Good luck, mate.

Teddy Good luck.

Rod Congratulations, Mrs Baron-to-be.

Erin Thank you.

Rod Cheery-bye.

Teddy Toodle-oo.

Rod Do you think you're Dick van fucking Dyke or something?

Rod and Teddy leave.
Baron stands and watches them go.
Erin goes and sits down beside Beattie.

Erin It's a new dawn.

Beattie I'll believe that when I see it, wee pet.

Erin That's what they're saying on the news. 'Change is in the air.'

Beattie The more things change, the more things stay the same.

Erin (*indicating his bottle*) You could do with making a few changes.

Beattie You're not wrong, wee love. One of these days.

Beattie sings, Christy Moore, 'Lock Hospital'.
DJ Cool enters.

DJ Cool Cheer up, man, it might never happen.

Beattie Perhaps it already has, did you ever think of that?

DJ Cool Whoa. Deep. You got me there.

Andy appears, wheeling a sleeping baby in a buggy.

Erin Uncle Beattie – I want you to tell me the truth now. It's had me worried sick – what actually happened last night?

Beattie What happened? Nothing happened. Nothing at-all at-all. (*He goes back to his paper.*) 'Whatever,' as you young folk might say. 'Whatever.'

DJ Cool As I heard it, Simon and your Baron ran into each other outside Lavery's and had a bit of a face-off –

Baron Oh, enough of that, I'm sick of hearing about it all.

Baron leaves.

DJ Cool They ran into each other outside Lavery's and Simon started having a go, the way he does, only this time he went a bit too far, said a few things he really shouldn't have –

Beattie Oh, it's all stuff and nonsense, all of it.

DJ Cool Alright, Victor Meldrew, keep your hair on. Simon's got it into his head that he and you, Erin, are madly in love. Do you know he's been ringing the station every night trying to get me to put him on air! Oh, you can't blame him. Love is a form of madness – it's scientifically proven. It was the same when I met Marianne. You're very like Marianne, you know. Always in your own world. But kinder – you're kinder, Erin. Not that my Marianne isn't kind. That's not what I mean at all. I love my Marianne to bits.

A car horn blasts.

Erin (*jumps*) God, that made me jump out of my skin. Everything's making me jumpy today.

Pause.

So. My bags are packed. I'm all ready to go. This time tomorrow we'll be married, and spending our first night together in our new flat, and then our new life will begin. I'm going to do a course, did I tell you, hairdressing maybe, or maybe to be a beautician. It's a whole new start. I couldn't be happier.

Pause.

The Baron's so old-fashioned, not wanting us to live together before we're man and wife, wanting to carry me over the threshold, all the rest of it. It's kind of romantic, I think.

DJ Cool Your head's in the clouds – both of you. Reality's going to bite and it's gonna bite hard. But good luck to you both – that's what I say. I mean it. Good luck.

Beattie Ach, wee love, my wee pet, you're flying the nest. I wish you the wind beneath your wings.

Pause.

DJ Cool So here we are. 'A new dawn.' That's what they're saying. 'A new dawn.' What's the saying? 'The darkest hour is just before the dawn.' Well, it's almost over and we can all start to move on. Draw a line under it all. (*Pause.*) Who knows what the future has in store? 'A new dawn.' (*Pause.*) Marianne is a good, kind, faithful woman. I love her with all of my heart and I know her better than anyone and I wouldn't change a thing.

Inside the house, Baron is playing Nick Drake, 'Northern Sky', and singing.

Erin This time tomorrow, I won't ever sit here again, listening to him play, wondering . . . It'll all have happened. It'll all be over.

Marianne crosses the stage, quietly, in the background. Baron plays and sings.

DJ Cool Still no Orla.

Erin No. She missed the whole thing. She's so busy these days with the music school. She's done well for herself. She'll never leave now. I've accepted it, too, you know: that I'm never going to America. It just isn't meant to be. I can't even tell you how hard it's been, stuck here, Orla never even around . . . I promised myself, the next time the Baron asks me to marry him . . . I went over and over it in my head. He's kind, I told myself, everyone says that, it's the first thing anyone ever says about him, what kind eyes he's got. I'll say yes, I said. And he asked, and I looked at him, and I thought it's true, he does have kind eyes. And I said yes and it was like a massive weight had been lifted from my shoulders. And then yesterday, I don't even know what caused it, I just felt like this cold cold fear –

Beattie It's just 'cold feet', wee love.

Siu Jing (*through the window*) Orla's here!

DJ Cool Orla's here. Let's all have a drink.

> *DJ Cool and Erin leave.*
> *Beattie sings 'Lock Hospital'.*
> *Marianne approaches.*
> *Andy pushes the buggy.*

Marianne Look at you. Sitting there happy as Larry. Comfortable?

Beattie And why shouldn't I be?

Marianne (*sits down*) No reason.

> *Pause.*

We call you 'Uncle Beattie', but you're not even our uncle. Did you love Mum?

Beattie Very much.

Marianne Did she love you?

> *Pause.*

Beattie To tell you the truth – I couldn't tell you.

Marianne Mum used to call Dad 'her man'. 'My man,' she used to say. 'Is that my man?'

Beattie Not yet.

Marianne When you have to snatch at whatever scraps of happiness you can get, and when that happiness by rights belongs to someone else – it takes its toll. Bit by bit you get harder – more cynical. But inside, I'm dying. (*She looks at Andy.*) Look at our Andy there. Just look at him. Once upon a time there were four children, and when their mother died they were turned into swans. For years and years they suffered, flying over and over the lake, tied together with silver chains, and they dreamed of when they'd be free. But when the bell finally tolled and the spell was broken, they were old, withered people, and they crumbled one by one to dust. The End. Hi, Andy.

Andy When are they going to stop making such a racket!

Beattie It'll all be over soon. (*Takes off his watch and winds it up; it chimes.*) This watch belonged to my grandfather, you know. (*Sings.*) 'Ninety years without slumbering, tick-tock, tick-tock, his life seconds numbering, tick-tock, tick-tock . . .' Never thought I'd be an old man myself.

Pause.

One of these days I'll set off and see the world. Walk into a travel agent – passport in my hand, toothbrush in my pocket – round-the-world ticket, please.

Andy Where will you go?

Beattie Where will I go? Will it matter?

Pause.

Andy Something happened in town last night. Outside Lavery's. Everyone's talking about it, but I can't get to the bottom of what actually happened.

Beattie It's nothing. A wee bit of banter that went too far. That Simon one was spoiling for a fight. Said some things he shouldn't. Baron loses his temper. Simon threatens to blow the Baron's head off. (*Laughs.*) Thinks he's the Terminator, that boy. Not right in the head if you ask me. Anyhow, they arranged to settle it today, fair and square, once and for all. They're having a death-match.

Marianne A what?

Beattie A death-match.

Marianne A death-match?

Beattie Pistols at dawn. Or rather – (*Checks his watch.*) at seventeen hundred hours. Just about now, in fact. Enough time to get it over with and back to the barracks.

Pause.

Marianne I can't tell if you're pulling our legs or not.

Beattie I'm being deadly serious.

Marianne But one of them might get hurt – or killed.

Beattie They're soldiers. It's in the job description.

A distant shout.

That sounds like young Simon, right enough.

Pause.

Andy I can't believe you're just sitting there. If you're being serious – You should do something.

Beattie What's it to do with me? And tell me this, son: what difference would it make, in the grand scheme of things? We're born, we live, we die – sooner or later we're all wormfood.

Marianne You're so full of bullshit. You're everything that's wrong with this place. You're the reason it's been stuck in a rut for so many years. Just endless fucking bullshit.

She goes towards the house: stops.

I can't go in there. I can't stand another second of any of this. People, talking. When Alex gets here, call me.

She walks off. Looks up.

Oh look, the starlings are out. Swooping and dipping . . . They don't know how lucky they are.

She leaves.

Andy The house is going to be so empty soon. Orla's never here, now Erin's going. There won't be any soldiers visiting. No Marianne. And you'll be setting off to see the world. What'll I do?

Beattie You have your wife and kids.

Andy My wife and kids. Yes, I have my wife and kids. There's always my wife and kids. Look, don't go telling anyone this, but sometimes – it feels like they're millstones, you know? Or like – albatrosses. Slung around my neck. Dragging me down. I mean that in the nicest possible way. I mean don't get me wrong. I love them, of course I love them. Am I making any sense at all?

Beattie In light of my forthcoming departure, son – in case I wind up on an island in Tahiti where there's a line of topless girls doing the hula at me and I don't come home – here's my advice to you. Put on your best pair of boots and get walking. And don't stop. The further you get the better.

Andy Hah.

Beattie You think I'm joking?

Simon appears.

Simon Uncle Beattie: the hour is nigh.

Beattie That's me. (*To Andy.*) If anyone asks where I am, Andy-pandy, tell them I'm bound to be back before too long. Like a bad penny.

Simon Takes one to know one! What were you guffing on about this time, you old fart?

Beattie I'll old fart you.

Simon Yeah, sure you will. When are you going to kick the bucket?

Beattie I'll kick you where the sun don't shine if you don't shut up.

Simon Chill out! I'm only taking the mickey. I'm harmless – honest, guv. I just want to make him shit his pants a bit.

He takes out his Cool Water and sprays it liberally all over himself. The bottle runs dry: he throws it away.

A whole bottle, and I can still smell it. Smells like rotten corpse. It's coming from inside of me.

Pause.

'Be afraid . . . Be very afraid.'

Beattie If you say so.

Beattie and Simon leave.
Andy pushes the buggy.
Erin and Baron enter.
DJ Cool enters and exits looking for Marianne.

Baron Well he's got a spring in his step today.

Erin Can you blame him?

Pause.

'It's a new dawn.'

Baron Erin, love, there's something I have to –

Erin What do you mean? Where are you going?

Baron I just have to – I promised I'd say goodbye, to Rod and Teddy.

Erin But they left ages ago. Nick, what's going on? Why are you acting so weird? (*Pause.*) Are you going to tell me what happened last night?

Baron It'll only take a minute. I'll be back before you know it.

Kisses her.

You are the love of my life. Five years. I've been in love with you for five years now, and every day I think I can't possibly love you any more, and then I do. More and more, Erin. More and more and more. Look at you. I can't believe you're mine. You're going to be my wife. And I'm going to whisk you away and make our fortunes and we'll live happily ever after. There's just one minor thing. You're not in love with me.

Erin I might not be 'in' love with you, but – no, listen – I'm going to be your wife, aren't I, and I'm going to be – faithful to you, and we're going to make a life together. (*Starts crying.*) I've never been in love, not once, in the whole of my life. I've dreamed about it night and day, what it must be like – but it's like there's something missing. Some crucial part of me – it's just not there.

Pause.

Don't look so scared.

Baron I'm not scared. There's nothing in the world I'm scared of. The only thing that scares me is this missing part of you. The person who might find it. Say something to me.

93

Pause.

Say something.

Erin Like what?

She lays her head on his chest.

Baron Just say something.

Erin Like what? What do you want me to say?

Baron Just say something. Anything.

Erin Stop it! Seriously!

Pause.

Baron Isn't it funny when some tiny, inconsequential thing suddenly seems so important. Something you might have laughed at, any other day, suddenly knocks you for six. Oh, come on, Baron, come on, stop feeling sorry for yourself. D'you know, it feels like I'm seeing everything – those fir trees, those oak trees, those – what even are they – for the first time ever. Oh my God, it feels like they're staring back at me. They're like, come on, what are you going to do next? The whole of life is yours for the taking.

A shout.

I have to go now. Look, you see that tree, that one there – it's all dry and withered, but it's still swaying along in the breeze with the others. I reckon that's what death's like: even if you die, you're still here, in a way. Goodbye, then.

Kisses her.

All of the papers and things are on my desk, by the way, under the paperweight.

Erin I'm coming with you.

94

Baron No! No you are not!

He takes a step away and then stops.

Erin.

Erin Yes?

Baron I –

He is lost for words.

D'you know what, I didn't have my caffeine fix this morning. You wouldn't do me a coffee would you?

He leaves.
Erin stands for a while then goes to the back of the stage and sits on a swing.
Andy pushes the buggy.

Andy What's happened to me? Where has it all gone? How did it go so wrong? Everyone always said I'd go places – that's what they said. He's going places. But I haven't. I haven't gone anywhere. I haven't done anything. I'm just a petty, boring, useless, lazy, stupid miserable lump. I used to read – I used to think – I used to have intelligent things to say and people would listen. I can't remember the last time I read a book. I can't seem to read more than a paragraph these days. I'm no better than the rest of them – the ones I used to laugh at – the ones who never read a book, never go to the theatre – who are suspicious of anyone who thinks or acts or looks even a tiny bit different. The ones who insist that nothing's going to change, who make sure that nothing ever changes . . . Working themselves up into a fury about things that happened hundreds of years ago – fanning their own self-righteous flames – because they have nothing else, nothing – nothing to hope of, dream about, aspire to – They refuse to listen, refuse to see – refuse to know that they're totally blinded and crippled by their own prejudices – and they ram it down their children's throats so their children grow up the same fucking zombies as the rest of them and the cycle goes on and on and on –

And I'm no better. I used to think I was – but what have I ever done? I'm exactly the fucking same as the rest of them. I was meant to go places – to bring back new perspectives – to think new thoughts and do new things – and it's too late now. This place will never change. Not really. Not in my lifetime. No matter what they say. Underneath the treaties and beneath the handshakes the same hatreds will bubble and fester until finally they erupt again. It's up to you now. (*To the baby.*) It's up to you to make this country a better place. It's your responsibility. Your burden.

Siu Jing (*through the window*) Who's that guldering? Andy-pandy? What are you guldering about? You'll wake Sophie if you're not careful. You're such a useless lump! If you're going to gulder, give the buggy to someone else.

Andy I'm not guldering.

Siu Jing (*inside*) Bobby! Who's a cheeky rascal? Mummy's going to get you – Mummy's going to tickle you – Bobby – There's Auntie Orla. Say bye-bye to Auntie Orla! Cheery-bye!

Andy 'Put on your best pair of boots and get walking.'

Andy leaves, pushing the buggy.
Orla and Vershinin enter. Erin goes to them.

Vershinin Almost time to go.

Pause.

Well. Good luck, ladies. Either of you seen Marianne?

Erin Somewhere in the garden. I'll fetch her.

Vershinin Thank you. (*He looks at his watch.*) I haven't much time.

Erin leaves.

A new dawn. And here we are. They gave me a good lunch, up at Stormont. Speeches – handshakes – all the rest of it – I smiled and nodded and shook hand after hand but my heart was here, with you. I've grown so at home here.

Orla Will we see each other again?

Vershinin Probably not.

Pause.

My wife and girls aren't flying out to join me until next week – If anything happens, or they need anything –

Orla Of course. Don't worry about it.

Pause.

Once all the soldiers are off the streets maybe this place will be able to breathe again.

Pause.

Things don't work out the way we want. I never intended to have my own music school, but I do now. Which means there's no way I can go to America.

Vershinin Anyway, thank you for everything. I'm sorry if –
    I don't need to spell it out, I know. For once. Please don't think too badly of me.

Orla (*wipes her eyes*) Where's Mimi?

Vershinin Why do goodbyes never seem to get any easier? (*He laughs.*) It's a hard-knock life. The bigger picture. That's what it's always impossible to see, when you're in the midst of it. But even so, we must admit that things are getting better. Only a few years ago, who'd have thought we'd be where we are today? One day, everything will have worked out perfectly. (*He looks at his watch.*) I really have to go. This place won't know itself now that the Troubles are over. What will people do with themselves?

Pause.

Education is the key, of course. New horizons – et cetera. (*He looks at his watch.*) Right. I really have to go now.

Orla Here she is.

Marianne enters.

Vershinin I came to say –

Marianne No.

Vershinin – goodbye.

Marianne No. No.

Orla steps to the side to give them some privacy.

Vershinin Goodbye.

Marianne 'Goodbye', no – No, I won't –

A prolonged kiss.

Orla Come on . . .

Marianne sobs uncontrollably and clings to him.

Vershinin Write to me. Don't forget me . . . Come on now. I really have to go . . . Orla, take her, would you, I really have to go – I'm late already.

He kisses Orla on the cheek, kisses Marianne once more and leaves.

Orla Mimi . . . Come on now, Marianne. Come on.

DJ Cool enters.

DJ Cool Oh, don't worry about it, let her have a wee cry, it's good to get it out of the system. 'Better out than in', eh. Ach, Marianne. My wee Marianne. You are my wife and I love you and I understand you better than anyone – better than you do yourself. See – I'm not cross with you – and Orla here's my witness – we'll go back to the way we were and we'll never speak of this again, any of it. I promise.

Marianne, holding back sobs, sings The Velvet Underground, 'Pale Blue Eyes', the first lines of the second verse.

Orla Come on, Mimi. It's OK. Come on. Someone get her some water?

Marianne I'm fine.

DJ Cool She's fine. Good girl.

A distant shot is heard.
Marianne sings the final verse of 'Pale Blue Eyes'.
Erin passes her some water. She drinks.

Marianne It's over. My life's a failure. I don't need anything now. I'll calm down in a minute. Whatever . . . I can't seem to think straight.

Orla Come on, Mimi. Come on. You have to get a grip. Let's go inside.

Marianne I'm not going back in! (*Sobs, and controls herself.*) I'm never going back in there again.

Erin Let's just sit here for a bit. We don't need to talk, we can just sit. This time tomorrow I'll be gone, after all.

Pause.

DJ Cool Fella rang the station last night wanting a request. 'What song?' I asked. He couldn't remember the name. 'Who's it by?' He didn't know that either. 'Do you know any of the words?' 'No,' says he, 'but it goes a bit like this. 'Da-da-da-da da da.'

Marianne 'Da-da-da-da da da.'

DJ Cool 'Da-da-da-da da da.' And he couldn't carry a tune in a bucket.

Orla That's funny.

Marianne weeps.

Erin Come on, Mimi.

DJ Cool 'Da-da-da-da da da.'

Siu Jing enters.

Siu Jing Sophie has had her nap but now Bobby needs his. It never ends! Where's Andy? Andy needs to push him to sleep while I feed Sophie. (*To Erin.*) This time tomorrow, Erin! I'm going to miss you. Bobby and Sophie will, too. Sophie will probably be walking next time you see her. She let go of the sofa this morning and took two whole steps all by herself. It happened like that with Bobby, almost overnight.

Erin I'll miss them too. Everything's changing so fast.

Siu Jing Well, let me tell you, now that you're all gone there are going to be more changes round here. I'm going to cut down those trees, for a start. They take up too much light. It's not good feng shui to have this much shade. And that dead one is dangerous. In a storm it could fall straight on the house and crush us all. I'll plant flowers, lots and lots of flowers, there and there and there – scented flowers – it will be like heaven. You won't recognise the place. (*Pause. Softly.*) It's a strange thing, you know. You leave a place . . . and it leaves you, too. It leaves you behind. Look at Hong Kong. The place I was born . . . no longer exists. I can't tell you how far away I felt, watching the fireworks and the celebrations of the handover on the news. The distance is not just space. It is time, too. I can never go home. I'd never really understood that before.

Pause.

But I'm losing the run of myself. I need to find Andy.

Siu Jing leaves, calling for Andy.
Pause.

Marianne We should get going too. Where's my coat?

DJ Cool Inside. I'll get it now.

DJ Cool leaves.

Orla Yes, we should all make a move.

They sit.
Beattie enters.

Beattie Orla!

Orla What is it?

Pause.

What is it?

Beattie I don't know how to say this.

Orla Oh God. What's happened?

Beattie I've had enough of it. I had enough of it all long ago. It's senseless, all of it. Senseless.

Marianne What's happened?

Beattie Erin – my poor wee Erin.

Erin What? For God's sake just get it over with. (*She weeps.*)

Beattie The Baron's just been shot. He's dead.

Erin I knew. I knew.

Beattie moves away and sits down with a newspaper.

Beattie Let them have a wee cry, it'll be good for them.

Sings the chorus of 'Lock Hospital'.

I wonder why the 'white laurels'. Must mean something. Whatever . . .

The three sisters stand, holding each other.

Marianne It's just us now. It's just us. 'A new dawn'. We have to start again, too. Somehow, we have to – start believing it's possible.

Erin One day we'll look back on this and it'll all make sense. We just have to get through each day now, one at a time.

Orla The days will pile up like grains of sand – they won't seem worth anything at the time, but then you'll look back and they'll have buried everything. All the pain, all the suffering – all of it buried. And once the past is laid to rest, people will be able to move on. It just takes time . . . That's what we need, now – time. That's what this country needs . . . Time doesn't heal, it just – obliterates. 'They lived through a great moment in history,' people will say, and that's what we'll be to them – all of us, all of our sorrows and secrets and loves and losses – that's what our lives will have meant: that we lived through it all, that we carried on, that we endured. We'll be long gone by then . . . But in the meantime we've got our own lives to live! We mustn't lose sight of that – we mustn't. We have to live our lives as best we can! And if we can hold out just a little longer – maybe we will know what all the suffering meant. If only we could know for sure!

DJ Cool enters with Marianne's coat.
Andy enters pushing a different buggy.

Beattie (*sings the second verse of 'Lock Hospital'*)
Whatever, whatever, as the young folks say. Whatever.

Orla If only we could know for sure. If only!'